First World War
and Army of Occupation
War Diary
France, Belgium and Germany

37 DIVISION
112 Infantry Brigade,
Brigade Machine Gun Company
24 February 1916 - 28 February 1918

WO95/2538/4

The Naval & Military Press Ltd
www.nmarchive.com
Published in association with The National Archives

Published by

The Naval & Military Press Ltd

Unit 10 Ridgewood Industrial Park,

Uckfield, East Sussex,

TN22 5QE England

Tel: +44 (0) 1825 749494

www.naval-military-press.com

www.nmarchive.com

This diary has been reprinted in facsimile from the original. Any imperfections are inevitably reproduced and the quality may fall short of modern type and cartographic standards.

© Crown Copyright
Images reproduced by permission of The National Archives, London, England, 2015.

Contents

Document type	Place/Title	Date From	Date To
Heading	WO95/2538/4		
Heading	37th Division 112th Infy Bde 112th Machine Gun Coy Mar 1916-Feb 1918		
Heading	112th Brigade. 37th Division. Company Disembarked Havre 2.3.16 112th Machine Gun Company 24.2.16 to 31st March 1916		
War Diary	Grantham	24/02/1916	24/02/1916
War Diary	Southampton	24/02/1916	01/03/1916
War Diary	Le Havre	02/03/1916	03/03/1916
War Diary	Doullens	04/03/1916	04/03/1916
War Diary	Authieule	04/03/1916	04/03/1916
War Diary	Orville	04/03/1916	04/03/1916
War Diary	Bienvillers Au Bois	04/03/1916	19/03/1916
War Diary	Souastre	20/03/1916	31/03/1916
Miscellaneous	112 Machine Gun Company. War Diary Appendix I		
Heading	112th Brigade. 37th Division. 112th Machine Gun Company April 1916		
War Diary	Souastre	01/04/1916	09/04/1916
War Diary	Sus. St. Leger	10/04/1916	30/04/1916
Heading	112th Brigade 37th Division. 112th Machine Gun Company May 1916		
War Diary	Sus-St-Leger	01/05/1916	01/05/1916
War Diary	Bienvillers-Au-Bois	01/05/1916	04/05/1916
War Diary	Fonquevillers	10/05/1916	14/05/1916
War Diary	Bienvillers-Au-Bois	15/05/1916	15/05/1916
War Diary	Saulty	16/05/1916	27/05/1916
War Diary	Bienvillers Au-Bois	28/05/1916	31/05/1916
Heading	112th Brigade. 37th Division. Went With 112th Brigade To 34th Division 5th July 1916; Rejoined 37th Div 21st August 1916		
War Diary	Bienvillers Au-Bois	01/06/1916	09/06/1916
War Diary	Saulty	09/06/1916	19/06/1916
War Diary	Bienvillers-Au-Bois	19/06/1916	30/06/1916
Heading	112th Brigade. 37th Division. Company Joined 34th Division 6th July 1916 Rejoined 37th Division 21st August 1916		
Heading	War Diary Of 112 Machine Gun Company From July 1st To July 31st 1916 Volume V		
War Diary	Bienvillers Au-Bois	01/07/1916	03/07/1916
War Diary	Halloy	04/07/1916	05/07/1916
War Diary	Millencourt	06/07/1916	08/07/1916
War Diary	Usna Tara	09/07/1916	16/07/1916
War Diary	Albert	17/07/1916	18/07/1916
War Diary	Bresle	19/07/1916	19/07/1916
War Diary	La Houssoye	20/07/1916	29/07/1916
War Diary	Bresle	30/07/1916	30/07/1916
War Diary	Becourtwood	31/07/1916	31/07/1916
Heading	112th Brigade. 34th Division Rejoined 37th Division 37th Division 22nd August 1916 112th Brigade Machine Gun Company August 1916		

War Diary	Becourt Wood	01/08/1916	06/08/1916
War Diary	S.13.b.9.8	07/08/1916	07/08/1916
War Diary	Bazentin le Petit Wood	07/08/1916	15/08/1916
War Diary	La Houssoye	16/08/1916	16/08/1916
War Diary	Longpre Corps-Saints	18/08/1916	18/08/1916
War Diary	Neuf Berquin	20/08/1916	20/08/1916
War Diary	Bruay	22/08/1916	25/08/1916
War Diary	Mazingabe	25/08/1916	31/08/1916
Heading	112th Brigade 37th Division. 112th Machine Gun Company September 1916		
War Diary	Mazingabe	01/09/1916	01/09/1916
War Diary	Noeux Les Mines	02/09/1916	02/09/1916
War Diary	Dieval	03/09/1916	19/09/1916
War Diary	Bully-Grenay	19/09/1916	30/09/1916
Heading	112th Brigade. 37th Division. 112th Machine Gun Company October 1916		
Heading	War Diary Of 112 Machine Gun Coy 1st Of October To 31st October 1916		
War Diary	Bully Grenay	01/10/1916	14/10/1916
War Diary	Verdrel	15/10/1916	15/10/1916
War Diary	Dieval	16/10/1916	16/10/1916
War Diary	Foufflin-Ricametz	18/10/1916	19/10/1916
War Diary	Petit Bouret	20/10/1916	20/10/1916
War Diary	Longuevillette	21/10/1916	21/10/1916
War Diary	Sarton	22/10/1916	22/10/1916
War Diary	Mailley	23/10/1916	23/10/1916
War Diary	Maillet Orville	30/10/1916	30/10/1916
War Diary	Roullens	31/10/1916	31/10/1916
Heading	112th Brigade. 37th Division. 112th Machine Gun Company November 1916		
War Diary	Doullens	01/11/1916	11/11/1916
War Diary	Vauchelles	12/11/1916	12/11/1916
War Diary	Bertrancourt	13/11/1916	13/11/1916
War Diary	Mailly Maillet	14/11/1916	17/11/1916
War Diary	Englebelmer	18/11/1916	25/11/1916
War Diary	Mailly-Maillet	26/11/1916	26/11/1916
War Diary	Louvencourt	27/11/1916	28/11/1916
War Diary	Robempre	30/11/1916	30/11/1916
Heading	112th Brigade. 37th Division. 112th Machine Gun Company December 1916		
War Diary	Rubempre	01/12/1916	15/12/1916
War Diary	Beauval	14/12/1916	14/12/1916
War Diary	Villier Le Hopital	15/12/1916	15/12/1916
War Diary	Blangemont	16/12/1916	16/12/1916
War Diary	Anvin	17/12/1916	17/12/1916
War Diary	Bellery	18/12/1916	18/12/1916
War Diary	Laleau	19/12/1916	20/12/1916
War Diary	Sloane Square	21/12/1916	31/12/1916
Heading	War Diary of 112 Machine Gun Coy 1st of January to 31st of January Volume XI		
War Diary	Sloane Square	01/01/1917	31/01/1917
Miscellaneous	H.Q. 12th Inf. Bde./Herewith	01/02/1917	01/02/1917
War Diary	Veille Chapelle	01/02/1917	08/02/1917
War Diary	Les Brebis	09/02/1917	28/02/1917
Heading	War Diary of 112th Machine Gun Company 1st of March To 31st Of March 1917 Volume XIII		

War Diary	Les Brebis	01/03/1917	03/03/1917
War Diary	Verquineul	04/03/1917	04/03/1917
War Diary	Robecq	05/03/1917	05/03/1917
War Diary	Nedonchelle	06/03/1917	08/03/1917
War Diary	Antin	09/03/1917	09/03/1917
War Diary	Rebreuviette	10/03/1917	18/03/1917
War Diary	Houvigneul	19/03/1917	31/03/1917
Heading	War Diary of 112th/37 Machine Gun Company 1st of April To 30th of April 1917 (Volume XIV)		
Miscellaneous	H.Q. 112th Inf Bde.	01/05/1917	01/05/1917
War Diary	Houvigneul	01/04/1917	05/04/1917
War Diary	Habarcq	06/04/1917	08/04/1917
War Diary	Warlus	09/04/1917	11/04/1917
War Diary	Arras	12/04/1917	12/04/1917
War Diary	Wanquetin	14/04/1917	14/04/1917
War Diary	Denier	15/04/1917	18/04/1917
War Diary	Noyellette	19/04/1917	22/04/1917
War Diary	Le Point De Jour	23/04/1917	27/04/1917
War Diary	In The Line	28/04/1917	29/04/1917
War Diary	Arras	30/04/1917	30/04/1917
Map	Edition 4. A Trenches		
Miscellaneous			
Heading	War Diary of 112th Machine Gun Company 1st of May 1917 To 31st May 1917 (Volume XV)		
War Diary	Denier	01/05/1917	13/05/1917
War Diary	Montenescourt	16/05/1917	16/05/1917
War Diary	Tilloy	19/05/1917	31/05/1917
Map	Trench Map		
Heading	War Diary of 112th Machine Gun Company 1st of June 1917 To 30th of June 1917 Volume XVI		
Miscellaneous	H.Q. 112th Inf Bde.	30/06/1917	30/06/1917
War Diary	Arras	01/06/1917	01/06/1917
War Diary	Agnes-Les Duisans	02/06/1917	07/06/1917
War Diary	Monneville	08/06/1917	10/06/1917
War Diary	Delettes	11/06/1917	23/06/1917
War Diary	Boeseghem	24/06/1917	24/06/1917
War Diary	La Brearde	25/06/1917	25/06/1917
War Diary	Locre	26/06/1917	29/06/1917
War Diary	Kemmel	30/06/1917	30/06/1917
Heading	War Diary of 112th Machine Gun Company 112th Machine Gun Company 1st of July To 31st of July 1917 (Volume XVII)		
War Diary	Kemmel	01/07/1917	01/07/1917
War Diary	Dranoutre	02/07/1917	12/07/1917
War Diary	Donegal Farm	13/07/1917	19/07/1917
War Diary	Bully Beef Farm	20/07/1917	25/07/1917
War Diary	Tyrone Farm	26/07/1917	31/07/1917
Heading	War Diary 112th M.G. Coy Aug 1917 Vol 18		
Heading	War Diary of 112th Machine Gun Company 1st of August 1917 To 31st of August 1917 (Volume XVIII)		
War Diary	Tyronne Farm	01/08/1917	01/08/1917
War Diary	Dranoutre	02/08/1917	05/08/1917
War Diary	La Polka	06/08/1917	06/08/1917
War Diary	Kemmel	07/08/1917	08/08/1917
War Diary	Kemmel Chateau	09/08/1917	28/08/1917
War Diary	Kemmel (Le Chateau)	29/08/1917	30/08/1917

War Diary	Kemmel	31/08/1917	31/08/1917
Heading	War Diary of 112th Machine Gun Company 1st Of September To 30th September 1917 (Volume XIX)		
Miscellaneous	112th Inf. Bde.	01/12/1917	01/12/1917
War Diary	In Camp Near Siege Farm	01/09/1917	13/09/1917
War Diary	Westoutre	14/09/1917	25/09/1917
War Diary	Shrewsbury Forest Sector	26/09/1917	30/09/1917
Heading	War Diary of 112th Machine Gun Company 1st October To 31st October 1917 (Volume XX)		
Miscellaneous	112th Inf Bde	01/11/1917	01/11/1917
War Diary	Willebeek Camp N9b (28 S.W 1/2000)	01/10/1917	04/10/1917
War Diary	In The Line	06/10/1917	25/10/1917
War Diary	Locre	26/10/1917	31/10/1917
Heading	War Diary Of 112th Machine Gun Company From 1st November 1917 To 30th November 1917 (Volume XXI)		
Miscellaneous	H.Q. 112th Inf Bde.	30/11/1917	30/11/1917
War Diary	Locre	01/11/1917	04/11/1917
War Diary	Ypres-Comines Canal Sector	08/11/1917	30/11/1917
Heading	War Diary of 112th Machine Gun Company 1st of December To 31st of December 1917 (Volume XXII)		
Miscellaneous	H.Q. 112th Inf Bde	01/01/1918	01/01/1918
War Diary	Seige Farm	01/12/1917	10/01/1918
War Diary	Lynde	11/01/1918	23/01/1918
War Diary	Renescure	24/01/1918	31/01/1918
Heading	War Diary of 112th Company M.G.C. From 1st February 1918 to 28th February 1918 (Volume XXIV)		
War Diary	Renescure	01/02/1918	13/02/1918
War Diary	La Cuytte Camp	14/02/1918	15/02/1918
War Diary	Maida Camp (Lafe Belge)	16/02/1918	19/02/1918
War Diary	Forester Camp	20/02/1918	25/02/1918
War Diary	Maida Camp (Cafe Belge)	26/02/1918	28/02/1918

W095/2538/4

37TH DIVISION
112TH INFY BDE

112TH MACHINE GUN COY
MAR 1916 - FEB. 1918

112th Brigade.
37th Division.

Company disembarked HAVRE 2.3.16.

112th MACHINE GUN COMPANY

24.2.16 to 31st MARCH 1 9 1 6

Feb 18

WAR DIARY
or
INTELLIGENCE SUMMARY.

(Erase heading not required.)

112 M.G. Coy

Army Form C. 2118.

Instructions regarding War Diaries and Intelligence Summaries are contained in F.S. Regs., Part II. and the Staff Manual respectively. Title pages will be prepared in manuscript.

Place	Date	Hour	Summary of Events and Information	Remarks and references to Appendices
GRANTHAM	29.2.16	6 a.m.	The Company with full complement of Officers, N.C.O's & men including transport left its quarters, B LINES, BELTON PARK, GRANTHAM, proceeding to the MILITARY SIDING for the purpose of entraining. Heavy snow	
—"—	—"—	7a.m.	Entrained for SOUTHAMPTON.	
SOUTHAMPTON	—"—	5.15 p.m.	Reached SOUTHAMPTON and at once detrained. A detachment of 3 Officers 4 N.C.O.S & 51 men embarked on H.M.T. "MARGUERITA" (which sailed that evening). The remainder of the Company with transport embarking on H.M.T. "AUSTRALIND".	
—"—	1.3.16	6 p.m.	Sailed for LE HAVRE after having been detained at SOUTHAMPTON owing the sate of Embarkation.	
LE HAVRE	2.3.16	4 a.m.	Anchored outside Harbour at LE HAVRE.	
—"—	2.3.16	10 a.m.	Docked, & at once disembarked. Proceeded to REST CAMP No 2 SANVIC where on arrival we were met by the detachment which sailed on H.M.T. "MARGUERITA"	
—"—	3.3.16	6 a.m.	Left REST CAMP for GARE DES MARCHANDISES where the Company Entrained with half of No 111 MACHINE GUN COMPANY. Heavy rain.	
—"—	—"—	12.15 p.m.	Left LE HAVRE.	

T2134. Wt. W708—776. 500000. 4/15. Sir J.C. & S.

Army Form C. 2118.

WAR DIARY
or
INTELLIGENCE SUMMARY.
(Erase heading not required.)

Instructions regarding War Diaries and Intelligence Summaries are contained in F. S. Regs., Part II. and the Staff Manual respectively. Title pages will be prepared in manuscript.

Place	Date	Hour	Summary of Events and Information	Remarks and references to Appendices
DOULLENS	4.3.16	1.30 a.m.	Arrived at ~~Authieule~~ DOULLENS where the Company detrained & marched into billets at AUTHIEULE arriving there at 6.30 a.m.	
AUTHIEULE	4.3.16	11.30 a.m	Marched from billets for BIENVILLERS to join 112 INFANTRY BRIGADE. Route followed: AUTHIEULE – AMPLIER – ORVILLE – THIEVRES – PAS – HENU – SOUASTRE – BIENVILLERS AU BOIS.	See attached
ORVILLE	4.3.16	12.45 p.m	A halt was ordered by a Staff Major 37th DIVISION for the purpose of shoeing eight mules and three horses, proceeding again at 2.20 p.m.	
BIENVILLERS AU BOIS	4.3.16	9 p.m.	The Company reached billets at BIENVILLERS, transport being parked for the night in the village	
– " –	5.3.16	10 p.m	The Company transport (and riding horses) was sent by order of 112 INFANT. BY BRIGADE to POMMIER where billets were found for transport Officer, drivers & grooms & lines for transport horses & mules.	
– " –	6.3.16		Three days were spent in Company training. On 6.3.16 the Company was inspected by Major General Count GLEICHEN K.C.V.O. C.B. C.M.G. D.S.O. On 9.3.16 & 10.3.16 work was carried on by two sections on wire entanglements	
	7.3.16			
	8.3.16			
	9.3.16			
	10.3.16			

WAR DIARY or INTELLIGENCE SUMMARY.

Army Form C. 2118.

Place	Date	Hour	Summary of Events and Information	Remarks and references to Appendices
BIENVILLERS AU BOIS	11.3.16 12.3.16 13.3.16 14.3.16 15.3.16		on the DIVISIONAL SECOND LINE, between FONCQUEVILLERS and HANNESCAMP. On these days work was continued on the three Gun Emplacements in the DIVISIONAL SECOND LINE before referred to. On the night of the 14.3.16 a Sub. of No 3 Section – 6071 Pte A. JONES was severely wounded by shrapnel on the BIENVILLERS – AU – BOIS – FONCQUEVILLERS road.	
BIENVILLERS AU BOIS	16.3.16 17.3.16		On these dates work was continued on the three machine Gun Emplacements already referred to. On the 16th inst., Pte A. JONES wounded on 14.3.16 died of his wounds in the 1/3 S. MIDLAND DIVISION FIELD AMBULANCE at COUIN.	
BIENVILLERS AU BOIS	18.3.16	5.30 p.m.	The two Sections working on the Machine Gun Emplacements were relieved by two Sections of No 11 MACHINE GUN COMPANY, this Company taking over the duties of 112 MACHINE GUN COMPANY on the relief of the 112th INFANTRY BRIGADE by the 11th INFANTRY BRIGADE. The relief of these two Sections was completed at 7 p.m.	
—	19.3.16	9 a.m.	The Company left its quarters marching to SOUASTRE, arriving there and	

WAR DIARY
or
INTELLIGENCE SUMMARY.
(Erase heading not required.)

Army Form C. 2118.

Place	Date	Hour	Summary of Events and Information	Remarks and references to Appendices
SOUASTRE	20.3.16		Taking over billets. This was completed by 11 a.m.	
-"-	21.3.16			
-"-	22.3.16			
-"-	23.3.16			
-"-	25.3.16			
-"-	26.3.16		This period was spent in further Company training.	
-"-	27.3.16			
-"-	28.3.16			
-"-	29.3.16			
-"-	30.3.16			
-"-	31.3.16			

112 MACHINE GUN COMPANY.

WAR DIARY

APPENDIX I

The march from AUTHIEULE to BIENVILLIERS AV BOIS on 4th March 1916 was carried out under adverse circumstances. The distance between AUTHIEULE & BIENVILLIERS is about 13 miles over a very hilly road which on the day in question, for the last six miles was covered with several inches of slush. Owing to the fact that both the Section Officers & most of the men had been either on board ship or on the train since the beginning of February 24th, the march proved a very severe test for the Company & it was with the greatest difficulty that the march was completed.

The chief points brought out on the march were four:-

   (a) The need of a field cooker.
   (b) The need of two mules on the ammunition limbers.
   (c) The need of an extra limber to carry H.Q. material.
   (d) The need of spare mules.

(a) Owing to the fact that the Company drew an unmarked ration it was impossible to give the men a meal on the march, with the result that they marched from 11.30 a.m. till 7.30 p.m. with nothing to eat. A meal, or even a drink of tea halfway would have made a great difference to the staying power of the men.

(b) It was found that two mules were not sufficient to draw the ammunition limbers, one of which had to be left behind at SOASTRE as the mules were incapable of finishing the march.

(c) An additional limber for H.Q. Equipment would enable the load on the ammunition limbers to be reduced & would greatly assist unloading at change of billets, as our H.Q. Equipment could be got away whilst other units were still unloading.

(d) It was found that the mule drawing the cooks cart was hot or in good enough condition to do its work. Consequently a mule had to be taken from one of the limbers to replace it, thus weakening of the Gun limber teams.

D. J. Armstrong 2/Lt

112th Brigade.
37th Division.

112th MACHINE GUN COMPANY

APRIL 1 9 1 6

WAR DIARY
or
INTELLIGENCE SUMMARY.

Army Form C. 2118.

Place	Date	Hour	Summary of Events and Information	Remarks and references to Appendices
SOUASTRE	1.4.16	12 noon	The Company was inspected, with its transport by the Divisional Commander Major General COUNT GLEICHEN K.C.V.O. C.B. C.M.G. D.S.O.	A.R. Brooke Capt
—"—	2.4.16 3.4.16 4.4.16 5.4.16 6.4.16 7.4.16 8.4.16		These days were spent in Company training.	A.R. Brooke Capt
—"—	9.4.16		The Company was relieved by 110th MACHINE GUN COMPANY. This Company leaving SOUASTRE at 12 noon for SUS-St-LEGER arriving there at 3-45 p.m. 9.4.16.	A.R. Brooke Capt
SUS-St LEGER	10.4.16 11.4.16 12.4.16 13.4.16 14.4.16 15.4.16 16.4.16 17.4.16 18.4.16 19.4.16		These days were spent in Company training.	A.R. Brooke Capt
—"—	19.4.16 to 30.4.16		This period was spent in Company training.	A.R. Brooke Capt O/C. 112th Machine Gun Company

112th Brigade
37th Division.
6---------------

112th MACHINE GUN COMAPNY

M A Y   1 9 1 6

WAR DIARY
or
INTELLIGENCE SUMMARY.
(Erase heading not required.)

Army Form C. 2118.

B. Hal Puckle Major O.C.
No. 112 M. GUN COMPANY.

Place	Date	Hour	Summary of Events and Information	Remarks and references to Appendices
SUS-ST LEGER	1.5.16	12.30 pm	The Company marched from its quarters at SUS-ST-LEGER to BIENVILLERS-AU-BOIS. The route taken was: SUS-ST-LEGER-MARLUZEL-COUTURELLE-SAULTY-HUMBERCAMP-BIENVILLERS. HUMBERCAMPS was reached at 4 p.m. where the Company halted for a meal and transport was parked. The march was continued from HUMBERCAMPS at 6.30 p.m. to meet BIENVILLERS-AU-BOIS might be reached after dusk according to orders received from the 112th INFANTRY BRIGADE. Transport was left at HUMBERCAMPS where time was allotted to it.	W. Short ¾
BIENVILLERS-AU-BOIS	1.5.16	8 pm	BIENVILLERS-AU-BOIS was reached at this hour & billets taken over by the Company.	W. Short ⅔
"	2.5.16	7 pm	From 11th BRIGADE MACHINE GUN COMPANY. Nos 2, 3, 4 Sections proceeded to relieve three sections of the 11th BRIGADE MACHINE Gun COMPANY as follows: No 2 Section relieved one section of the 11th MACHINE GUN Company at HANNESCAMP. No 3 Section similarly relieved at FONQUEVILLERS and No 4 Section relieved a section on the FRONT LINE. No 2 & 3 sections both being in the DIVISIONAL LINE. The whole was complete by 6 p.m.	W. Short ⅔ 2/4

W. Hy Puckle O.C.
No. 112 M. GUN COMPANY.

WAR DIARY
or
INTELLIGENCE SUMMARY.
(Erase heading not required.)

Army Form C. 2118.

A. Huh. Vueb
Major
O.C.
No. 112 M. GUN COMPANY.

Place	Date	Hour	Summary of Events and Information	Remarks and references to Appendices
BIENVILLERS-AU-BOIS	3-5-16		No 4 Section was relieved of the position in the FRONT LINE & returned to Headquarters at BIENVILLERS-AU-BOIS.	A. Vhutz 2/Lt
—"—	4-5-16		No 1 Section took up positions in the village defences of BIENVILLERS-AU-BOIS. One Gun team of this section took up a position in TRENCH 86 which is in the support Line immediately in front of MONCHY.	A. Vhutz 2/Lt
—"—	4-5-16	2.30 am	At this hour after a heavy bombardment the GERMANS carried out a local raid on our trenches in front of MONCHY. The Emplacement in which the Gun team new lived above was heavily damaged and nearly fell in. This much was due to casualties. One man was pinned by an arm & nearly falling. Him on the head but his life was undoubtedly saved by the fact that he was wearing at the time one of the steel helmets that are being issued. The injury sustained was slight.	A. Vhutz 2/Lt
FONQUEVILLERS	10-5-16	1.3 pm	No. 3 Section was relieved at FONQUEVILLERS by the 137th BRIGADE MACHINE GUN COMPANY. The section returned to HANNESCAMPS where new position for emplacements was selected & work started on the same.	A. Vhutz 2/Lt
	10-5-16 12-5-16		Between these dates the work was carried on & considerable amount of instruction carried out on the GERMAN positions at MONCHY, LES ESSARTS, & GOMMECOURT.	A. Vhutz 2/Lt

A. Vhutz 2/Lt
O.C.
No. 112 M. GUN COMPANY.

Army Form C. 2118.

WAR DIARY
or
INTELLIGENCE SUMMARY.
(Erase heading not required.)

No. 112 M. GUN COMPANY.

O.C.

Place	Date	Hour	Summary of Events and Information	Remarks and references to Appendices
BIENVILLERS-AU-BOIS	18.5.16		On this date the Company was relieved by 110th MACHINE GUN COMPANY, which Company took over the billets of 112th MACHINE GUN COMPANY at BIENVILLERS-AU-BOIS. Relief was carried out by daylight & the Company relieved by sections, the following order:— No 2 SECTION, No 3 SECTION (both at HANNESCAMPS), No 4 SECTION (in reserve) and No 1 SECTION (VILLAGE DEFENCES at BIENVILLERS-AU-BOIS, and one gun team in the support line – TRENCH 26). On relief these sections marched independently to SAULTY where gun teams billets were taken over. The relief which was commenced at 10.45 a.m. was completed without incident at 2.15 p.m.	
SAULTY.	16.5.16 26.5.16		This period was spent in Company training.	
SAULTY.	27.5.16		The Company marched from its billets at SAULTY to relieve the 110th MACHINE GUN COMPANY at BIENVILLERS-AU-BOIS. Marching from SAULTY at 6.15 pm, the Company reached HUMBERCAMP at 7.50 p.m. From this point sections proceeded independently at intervals of a quarter of an hour in the order in which they were to relieve, i.e. No 4 SECTION (RIGHT SECTOR) relieving at 6.30 p.m., No 2 SECTION (CENTRE) No 1 SECTION (LEFT) & No 3 SECTION (RESERVE). The relief was completed. W. [signature] O.C. No. 112 M. GUN COMPANY.	

Army Form C. 2118.

WAR DIARY
or
INTELLIGENCE SUMMARY.
(Erase heading not required.)

B. Del Queck _____ O.C.
No. 112 M. GUN COMPANY.

Instructions regarding War Diaries and Intelligence Summaries are contained in F. S. Regs., Part II. and the Staff Manual respectively. Title pages will be prepared in manuscript.

Place	Date	Hour	Summary of Events and Information	Remarks and references to Appendices
BIENVILLERS AU-BOIS	26.5.16 31.5.16		Without incident to 11.10 p.m. The Transport remained in lines at LA CAUCHIE. During this period, work on Emplacements was carried out by sections. On several occasions indirect fire was brought to bear on MONC HY.AU. BOIS. On the night of the 30th 8,000 rounds were fired into Monchy from guns in each of the three sectors held by the Company.	W.J.Hunt W.J.Hunt

W.J.Hunt Capt. O.C.
No. 112 M. GUN COMPANY.

112th Brigade.
37th Division.

Went with 112th Brigade to 34th Division
5th July 1916; Rejoined 37th Div 21st August 1916

112th MACHINE GUN COMPANY

JUNE 1916

Army Form C. 2118.

WAR DIARY
or
INTELLIGENCE SUMMARY.
(Erase heading not required.)

P. M. L. Pickthages
NO. 112 M. GUN COMPANY.

Instructions regarding War Diaries and Intelligence Summaries are contained in F. S. Regs., Part II. and the Staff Manual respectively. Title pages will be prepared in manuscript.

Place	Date	Hour	Summary of Events and Information	Remarks and references to Appendices
BIENVILLERS AU-BOIS	1.6.16 to 8.6.16		Between these dates work was carried on constructing Emplacements. Nothing of importance occurred.	
— " —	8.6.16		The Company was relieved by 110th MACHINE GUN COMPANY & returned to SAULTY. The relief which commenced at 5.30 p.m. was completed without incident at 11.45 p.m.	K.J. Stores
SAULTY	9.6.16 to 19.6.16		Between these dates the company furnished working parties for the ABRET P?PONMIER light Railway. Company training was carried on also	Army Rules
BIENVILLERS -AU-BOIS.	19.6.16		The Company relieved the 110th MACHINE GUN Company at BIENVILLERS-AU-BOIS. The relief which commenced at 8-30 am and was completed without incident.	Army Rules
-AU-BOIS.	20.6.16	at 12.45 AM	On this night fire was opened upon a hostile working party near the OSIER BEDS. 1000 rounds being expended. Range 1900 x. Time M/n No of guns 1.	Army Rules
	21.6.16		Dugouts was works upon and various alternative emplacements sighted.	
	24.6.16		Lines were laid out for fire L.R. direct and indirect upon Monchy Northern side of PIDGEON WOOD and Southern Exits from ESSARTS Village.	Army Rules
	25.6.16		En cooperating with artillery and Trench Mortars fire was brought to bear on MONCHY by 2 guns using indirect fire 2000 rounds being expended and	Army Rules

Army Form C. 2118.

B. Stah Preston
Major
O.C.
No. 112 M. GUN COMPANY.

WAR DIARY
or
INTELLIGENCE SUMMARY.
(Erase heading not required.)

Instructions regarding War Diaries and Intelligence Summaries are contained in F. S. Regs., Part II. and the Staff Manual respectively. Title pages will be prepared in manuscript.

Place	Date	Hour	Summary of Events and Information	Remarks and references to Appendices
BENVILLERS - ADBOIS	25.6.18		upon the NORTH edge of PIDGEON WOOD, 1000 rounds being fired by 2 guns using direct fire.	Benn Preston
	26.6.18		On this date eleven 12 guns were brought to bear upon the line MONCHY ESSARTS and PIDGEON WOOD. 4 guns were laid on the North of PIDGEON WOOD and traversed to the Left towards ESSARTS expending 5800 rounds. Four three guns firing on ESSARTS traversed right towards PIDGEON WOOD expending 9000 rounds. 4 guns fired into MONCHY TOWN enfilading various streets and co-operating with 111th M.G. Company on the Left. 10,500 rounds were then expended. The guns during this day fired intermittently but rapid fire was kept up during the intense artillery bombardment which commenced at 9.45 A.M.	Benn Preston
	27.6.18	9.45 AM 10.35 10.35 AM 6.25 p 7.55 p	Machine Guns cooperated with artillery sweeping targets as follows MONCHY - HANNES CAMPS Monchy Hannescamps roads from E.5.a.7.7 to W.30.c.4.0; E.5.b. 10.35 to W.29.b.80.10 and E.5.a.1. to E.5.a.9.6. No. 111 M.G. Company cooperated from the Left. Essarts Southern edges of ESSARTS and Northern end of PIDGEON WOOD were also engaged.	

Army Form C./2118.

B/112 Vickers M.G.O.C.
No. 112 M.G. COMPANY.

WAR DIARY
or
INTELLIGENCE SUMMARY.
(Erase heading not required.)

Instructions regarding War Diaries and Intelligence Summaries are contained in F. S. Regs., Part II. and the Staff Manual respectively. Title pages will be prepared in manuscript.

Place	Date	Hour	Summary of Events and Information	Remarks and references to Appendices
BIENVILLERS AU-BOIS.	27.6.16	6.30 P.M.	At 6.30 P.M. the enemy obtained a direct hit upon the M.G. emplacement in the General Support Trench between 85 Street and 86 Street, resulting in one casualty. The gun and tripod were undamaged and were moved to an alternative position.	
		7 P.M. & 8 P.M.	Between 7 P.M. and 8 P.M. artillery fire was brought to bear upon the guns on the right which retired to alternative emplacements without loss. 12,500 Rounds were fired into MONCHY and 8,500 into PIDGEON WOOD and ESSARTS.	Dan Piela
	28.6.16		14 guns cooperated with Trench Mortars and 111. M.G. Coy at daybreak and from 6.45 A.M. to 7.25 A.M. Alternative positions were taken up by the left section guns. Open emplacements were built during the night 28/29.6.16 in the front line trenches held by the R. Battalion. Rounds fired. MONCHY. 12,200. ESSARTS. 7,600.	
	29.6.16		Intermittent fire was kept up during the day and night upon PIDGEON WOOD, ESSARTS and MONCHY 27,250 rounds in all being fired of which 17,000 were fired into MONCHY. 12 guns in all being in action.	Dan Piela

Army Form C. 2118.

B Stak Puech West
No. 112 M. GUN COMPANY.

WAR DIARY
or
INTELLIGENCE SUMMARY.
(Erase heading not required.)

Instructions regarding War Diaries and Intelligence Summaries are contained in F. S. Regs., Part II. and the Staff Manual respectively. Title pages will be prepared in manuscript.

Place	Date	Hour	Summary of Events and Information	Remarks and references to Appendices
BENVILLERS-AU-BOIS	29.6.16		Emplacements (open) were completed in front of our front line (New Sap) for two VICKERS guns and made ready for the positions to be taken up immediately.	Danvillers
	30.6.16		Intermittent fire was kept up all day & night in cooperation with artillery when possible. 17,750 rounds were fired into MONCHY; 7000 into ESSARTS and ____ into PIDGEON WOOD.	Danvillers Lieut.

112th Brigade
34th Division.

Company joined 34th Division 6th July 1916
Rejoined 37th Division 21st August 1916;

112th MACHINE GUN COMPANY

JULY 1916

CONFIDENTIAL

Vol 5

WAR DIARY

OF

112 MACHINE GUN COMPANY

FROM

JULY 1st TO JULY 31st 1916

VOLUME V

[signature]
Lt & Adj
No. 112 MACHINE GUN COY.

Army Form C. 2118.

WAR DIARY
or
INTELLIGENCE SUMMARY.
(Erase heading not required.)

A. Dalrueth
May 6

Instructions regarding War Diaries and Intelligence Summaries are contained in F.S. Regs., Part II. and the Staff Manual respectively. Title pages will be prepared in manuscript.

Place	Date	Hour	Summary of Events and Information	Remarks and references to Appendices
BENVILLERS AU. BOIS.	1-7-16	7.30AM	12 guns cooperated with artillery and trench mortars. Targets MONCHY-AU-BOIS, ESSARTS and PIGEON WOOD. Fire was kept up intermittently	Denville
		16	all day. 2 gun pushed forward in front of NEW SAP. had orders to fire	
		M/N.	only on "living targets" did not fire and were withdrawn in the evening when 46th Division took over trenches.	
	2-7-16		12 Guns continued to fire intermittently on aforementioned targets.	
	2-7-16		3 guns fired during the night upon the "Z".	
	3-7-16		Guns fired as above during the day. During the afft and	
	4-7-16		evening the company were relieved by the 138th Coy - Relief complete with out incident at 12.35 AM 4-7-16	Denville
HALLOY			Company proceeded to HALLOY to billets and rest, where they had part of G.H.Q reserves.	
	5-7-16		Company remained in rest. Guns etc cleaned and all equipment overhauled.	
	6-7-16	1-30 PM	At 1-30 PM The Coy was placed in beheviaion & transported to MILLENCOURT, WEST of ALBERT where they bivouaced. Company	Denville
MILLENCOURT				

WAR DIARY
or
INTELLIGENCE SUMMARY.
(Erase heading not required.)

Army Form C. 2118.

No. 112 MACHINE GUN COMPANY

A. Val Pick? O.C.

Place	Date	Hour	Summary of Events and Information	Remarks and references to Appendices
MILLENCOURT	6.7.16		attached to 3rd Division	
	7.7.16	6 A.M.	Having reinforced the Company moved off at 6 A.M. to BELLEVUE FARM, EAST of ALBERT when Boraige got into touch with B.112 B. & M.Os they halted by road. BELLEVUE FARM — CEMETARY. The Company bivouaced for the night	
	8.7.16		Company remained in bivouac till 7 P.M. when they commenced to relieve 58th Company. Company HQs moved to USNA-TARA line EAST of ALBERT. Nos 2 & 3 Sections in the line at x.15.c.&.d. (Ref. 57000 Trench map) Quarter No 1 and 4 Sections in reserve at USNA-TARA. Relief completed without incident at 1 AM. Transport returns to camp & LONG VALLEY	
USNA TARA	9.7.16		Dispositions as yesterday — forward sections subjected to much shelling resulting in 5 Casualties or N.3 Section guns withdrawn to support line by 11 P.M. Transport at BECOURT WOOD.	
	10.7.16		6 Guns moved forward to SUNKEN ROAD. Casualties. Officer 1. Killed shell or. 1 Killed 1 wounded.	
	11.7.16		8 guns relieved by No 7 M.G. Coy, and new position taken up to right of original position resting on CONTALMAISON and Quarter	

WAR DIARY or INTELLIGENCE SUMMARY.

Army Form C. 2118.

B. Stel Puckty Major
O.C.

Place	Date	Hour	Summary of Events and Information	Remarks and references to Appendices
USNA-TARA	11-7-16		running through BAILIFF WOOD along SUNKEN ROAD towards POSIERES. Casualties Officers 1 killed 1 wounded. O.R. 1 killed, 4 wounded. HQrs remained at USNA-TARA line.	
	12-7-16		Enemy attempted Counterattack on CONTALMAISON but were stopped by artillery fire & m.g. fire. Two guns got into action but were shelled as target was not good. Right hand gun got good effect at range 2000x catching the enemy in mass & Elleguie fire. Casualties O.R. 2 wounded.	
	13-7-16		Same positions as above. No Casualties.	
	14-7-16		do	
	15-7-16		Same positions were held but during attack on POSIERES & extra guns were taken up & brought into action covering left flank of 112th Brigade. Two sections on either M.G. sub W. 9/1511 R° but new attempting by infantry on Right of 112 Brigade but were stopped by artillery fire. Casualties 1 or O. Ranks 1 killed 1 wounded.	
	16-7-16		RELIEF. Conference was taken without incident by 6th M.G. Coy. Harassed to ALBERT & billeted. Transport remained near BECOURT WOOD dump.	

Army Form C. 2118.

WAR DIARY
or
INTELLIGENCE SUMMARY.
(Erase heading not required.)

A Neil Puckle Major O.C.
No. 119 M. GUN COMPANY.

Instructions regarding War Diaries and Intelligence Summaries are contained in F.S. Regs., Part II. and the Staff Manual respectively. Title pages will be prepared in manuscript.

Place	Date	Hour	Summary of Events and Information	Remarks and references to Appendices
ALBERT	17.7.16		In billets at ALBERT. 2/Lieut HARRIS reported for duty.	Qua. Rules
	18.7.16		Reinforcements 20 O.R. reported for duty to replace casualties 17-8-16.	
BRESLE	19.7.16		Company moved to Bresle BRESLE arriving there at 9 P.M. and billetted.	Qua. Ques
LA HOUSSOYE	20.7.16		Company marched to LA HOUSSOYE arriving at 12 noon and billetted.	
	21.7.16		Company remained at LA HOUSSOYE refitting and company training etc.	
	22.7.16		" "	
	23.7.16		Reinforcements 24 other ranks reported	
	24.7.16		Brigade inspected by G.O.C. IIIrd Corps	
	25.7.16		Reinforcements 2/Lt PENMAN & PALMER reported. 112 Brigade inspected by G.O.C. 3rd Corps	
	26.7.16		" Practici were carried out on Rue Rouge.	
	27.7.16		" "	
	28.7.16		S.O.R. Reinforcements reported.	
	29.7.16		ditto	QuaRules
BRESLE	30.7.16		The Company on this date moved to BRESLE with the 112th Infantry Brigade and went into billets there.	

WAR DIARY
or
INTELLIGENCE SUMMARY.

(Erase heading not required.)

Army Form C. 2118.

A. Ehr Pueble O.C.
No. 112 M. G. COMPANY

Place	Date	Hour	Summary of Events and Information	Remarks and references to Appendices
BÉCOURT WOOD	31/7/16	6.55 PM	At 6.55 PM the Company marched via ALBERT and then went into bivouac near BÉCOURT Wood at Ref. 1/20000 Trench map W.30.d.2.2. and formed part of Brigade in Reserve.	

112th Brigade.
34th Division
Rejoined   37th Division 22nd August 1916

112th BRIGADE MACHINE GUN COMPANY

AUGUST 1 9 1 6 :::::

WAR DIARY
or
INTELLIGENCE SUMMARY.
(Erase heading not required.)

Army Form C. 2118.

B. Sek. Puchleh
O.C.
No. 9 COMPANY.

Place	Date	Hour	Summary of Events and Information	Remarks and references to Appendices
BECOURT WOOD.	1-8-16		Company was in bivouac at W.30.d.4.2 Ref. 57DSE. and remained till 6-8-16 in reserve. Drafts 30 other ranks joined for duty.	
	6-8-16		The Company relieved 101st M.G. Coy. on line between BAZENTIN-LE-PETIT WOOD and HIGH WOOD. Guns were placed in the following positions:—	
			No. 2 Section S.3.c.7.5	
			S.3.c.4½.4½	
			S.2.d.9.6	
			S.2.d.8.2½	
			No. 3 Section S.2.d.4½.1	
			S.2.d.1.2½	
			S.8.b.7.7½	
			S.8.a.8.7	
			The remaining 2 sections were in reserve at S.13 & 9 c. Casualties NIL.	
S.13.b.9.4 & 7.8.16			Guns at S.2.d.9.5 were moved to S.3.c.11.a The following strong points were garrisoned by the Company:—	[signature]

Army Form C. 2118.

WAR DIARY
or
INTELLIGENCE SUMMARY.
(Erase heading not required.)

No. 112 M. G...
O. C. Major

Place	Date	Hour	Summary of Events and Information	Remarks and references to Appendices
BAZENTIN LE PETIT WOOD	7.8.16		"A" Post S.13.6 & 6, by 2 Guns No. 1 Section	
			"B" Post S.7.d.2.1, by 2 guns No. 1 Section	
			"C." Post S.7.6.8.3½, by 1 gun No. 4 Section	
			"D" Post S.8.a.4.5 by 2 guns No. 4 Section	
			The 4th gun No 4 Section in D.O. at S.13.6.9.2. Casualties N.I.L.	
"	8.8.16		No change in positions. Casualties 1 Killed 2 Wounded O.R.	
"	9.8.16		Inter-Section relief carried out without incident. Casualties 1 wounded O.R.	
"	10.8.16		Casualties 1 O.R. wounded. All gun positions heavily shelled during evening and night 10th-11th	
"	11.8.16		Gun at S.3.c.1.1. was moved into newly cut lines intermediate line at S.2.d.8.5. 2 Guns at post 'D' were moved to S.7.6.9.2.4½ owing to post 'D' being heavily shelled. Casualties 1 O.R. wounded	
"	12.8.16		Gun at S.2.d.8.2.1 moved to S.8.B.5.2.9. Casualties 1.O.R. wounded.	
"	13.9.16		1 Gun destroyed by shell fire - Casualties 3 other ranks wounded.	
"	14.8.16		Inter section reliefs carried out without incident. Casualties 1 O.R killed 1 O R wounded 1 O.R Missing.	

T2134. Wt. W708—776. 500000. 4/16. Sir J. C. & S.

Army Form C. 2118.

B. Hal Puckeh
Major
O.C.

WAR DIARY
or
INTELLIGENCE SUMMARY.
(Erase heading not required.)

Instructions regarding War Diaries and Intelligence Summaries are contained in F.S. Regs., Part II. and the Staff Manual respectively. Title pages will be prepared in manuscript.

Place	Date	Hour	Summary of Events and Information	Remarks and references to Appendices
BAZENTIN LE PETIT WOOD.	15.8.16		The Company was relieved by the 101st M.G. Company and proceeded to private ground South of MAX REDOUBT. CASUALTIES 1 O.R. missing. From the 6th to 15.8.16 the Company were under continuous shell fire, all ranks shewing great steadiness.	
LA HOUSSOYE.	16.8.16		The Company and transport proceeded by road to LA HOUSSOYE where it went into billets remaining till 18.8.16	
LONGPRÉ - CORPS-SAINTS.	18.8.16		The Company on this date marched to FRECHINCOURT and entrained to LONGPRÉ-CORPS-SAINTS and billeted, remaining till 20th.	
NEUF BERQUIN	20.8.16		The Company entrained at LONGPRÉ and proceeded to BAILLEUL, detrained and marched into billets at NEUF BERQUIN remaining there till 22.8.16	
BRUAY	22.8.16		The Company marched into billets at BRUAY Rue Q.6.7, proceeding from LESTREM station by train to FOUQUEREUIL and thence by road.	
	23.8.16		Company remains at BRUAY in billets	
	24.8.16		The Company marched to MAZINGARBE and billets having attached to 20th Division.	
	25.8.16		The Company relieved 49th M.G. Coy at 14 Bis Line 100 S. Coy H.Q.s near	Beau Puits

T2134. Wt. W708—776. 500000. 4/15. Sir J. C. & S.

Army Form C. 2118.

B Nell Puckle
Major O.C.
...PANY.

WAR DIARY
or
INTELLIGENCE SUMMARY.
(Erase heading not required.)

Instructions regarding War Diaries and Intelligence Summaries are contained in F.S. Regs., Part II. and the Staff Manual respectively. Title pages will be prepared in manuscript.

Place	Date	Hour	Summary of Events and Information	Remarks and references to Appendices
MAZINGARBE	25.8.16		113⁰ Bde H.Qrs. 3 Sections in the line - 1 Section in reserve at Coy H.Q. Casualties Nil. Transport stationed at NOEUX-LES-MINES. Guns were placed in emplacements at points as follows	
			No.1 Section G.30.b.4.9; G.30.b.5.1; G.30.d.6.6; G.30.d.8.5	
			No.2 Section H.30.6.2.8; G.23.c.9.3; G.23.c.7.3; G.30.c.3.8	
			No.3 Section G.30.d.8.2; G.36.b.5.3; G.36.b.6.7; G.36.d.7.8	
			No.4 Section in reserve.	
	26.8.16		Relief passes completed without incident. All quiet in line. Casualties Nil.	
"	27.8.16		NORTHERN SAP REDOUBT shelled in afternoon by 4.5 How: and parapets knocked in. 1500 rounds fired on LIMBER DUMP RAILWAY at point near Casualties Nil.	
"	28.8.16		3000 rounds fired on LIMBER DUMP at point 19.d.9.6 by 2 guns of No.1 section. Work on dugouts carried on at Casualties Nil.	
"	28.8.16		No.1 and 3 Sections fired 4000 rounds from 4 guns on targets BOIS. DIX. HUIT and cross roads H.27.C.5.2 and H.33.c.1). Casualties Nil.	
"	29.8.16		Quiet all day and night. Casualties nil. Many trenches fell in during the night. [signature]	

Army Form C. 2118.

WAR DIARY
or
INTELLIGENCE SUMMARY.
(Erase heading not required.)

16 Del Puebla May

Place	Date	Hour	Summary of Events and Information	Remarks and references to Appendices
MAZINGARBE	29/8/16		on account of heavy rain.	
	30/8/16		Ammunition expended 2250 rounds. Targets Roads in vicinity of H.33.A and H.33.C. Casualties Nil.	
	31/8/16			
	31/8/16		Ammunition expended nil Casualties Nil	

DanMules
Lieut
113 MgCoy

112th Brigade
37th Division.

112th MACHINE GUN COMPANY

SEPTEMBER 1 9 1 6

WAR DIARY
or
INTELLIGENCE SUMMARY.
(Erase heading not required.)

Army Form C. 2118.

R. Stella Tuckh Major

No. 112 M. GUN COMPANY.

Place	Date	Hour	Summary of Events and Information	Remarks and references to Appendices
MAZINGARBE	1/9/16		The Company was relieved by 167th M.G. Company and proceeded to NOEUX-LES-MINES to billets.	
NOEUX-LES-MINES	2/9/16		The Company marched with the remainder of the 112th Infantry Brigade to billets at DIÉVAL.	
DIÉVAL	3/9/16		The Company carried out training etc. on line dates.	
	4/9/16			
	5/9/16			
	6/9/16		The Company was inspected by G.O.C. 37th Division. Company training was carried on. Transport inspection by O/C 37th Division road train. 1 Section was detached to HOUDAIN for anti aircraft purposes till 18/9/16	
	13/9/16		2 Sections detached for duty with 189 M.G. Company on LORETTE RIDGE. The Company marched into billets at HERSIN, and halted for the night. The Company being joined by one section detached on the 13/9/16 relieves the 1st & 18th M.G. Coys at BULLY-GRENAY. Two sections in the line Sectors ANGRES I and I - One Section at H.Q.s. The detached Section transferred to 63rd M.G. Coy and moved to FOSSE.10. Transport at Cambrin	
	18/9/16			
	19/9/16			

Army Form C. 2118.

B. Mc Veagh Lieut O.C.
No. 112 M. GUN COMPANY.

WAR DIARY
or
INTELLIGENCE SUMMARY.
(Erase heading not required.)

Place	Date	Hour	Summary of Events and Information	Remarks and references to Appendices
BULLY-GRENAY	19/9/16		HERSIN still - Coy HQs at BULLY-GRENAY.	
	20/9/16		Transport moved to FOSSE 10. The following gun positions were taken up. at Ref 10,000 Trench map M.19.d.4.4. M.19.d.6.1. M.19.d.7.2. M.#32.A.4.4. M.32.A.0.4.; R.23.d.4.2.; R.30.c.9.9. R.30.c.5.3. No casualties	
	21/9/16		No casualties - August	
	22/9/16		"	
	23/9/16		No Casualties. Rounds fired 1000. Targets ROLLINCOURT and LIEVIN	
	24/9/16		" " Rounds fired 2000 " ROLLINCOURT and LIEVIN and roads connecting. Also road between ROLLINCOURT CITÉ and FOSSE.	
	25/9/16		Casualties NIL. Rounds fired 2000. Targets ANGRES.	
	26/9/16		Guns at BULLY TRENCH considerably worried by minenwerfer. No casualties however and no damage done to emplacements. 1000 Rounds fired Targets M.27.B.2.6., Cité de ROLLINCOURT and M.26.D.8.3.	
	27/9/16		Casualties NIL. Rounds fired. 1000 M.27.B.2.5. ROLLINCOURT & M.26.B.3. 8.50 ANGRES. 250 LIEVIN ROAD. Total 2100 rounds	

[signature]

Army Form C. 2118.

B.Hd Qrs 1st Cup. O.C. COMPANY.
No. 112 M. 5O" COMPANY.

WAR DIARY
or
INTELLIGENCE SUMMARY.

(Erase heading not required.)

Instructions regarding War Diaries and Intelligence Summaries are contained in F. S. Regs., Part II. and the Staff Manual respectively. Title pages will be prepared in manuscript.

Place	Date	Hour	Summary of Events and Information	Remarks and references to Appendices
BULLY-GRENAY	27/9/16		Minenwerfer continued to fall close to BULLY TRENCH guns but no damage was done to emplacement.	
	28/9/16		Horse transport was heard ENE Eastern end of BULLY GRENAY trench at 9 P.M. 11 P.M. Casualties NIL. Rounds fired M 1500. ROLLINCOURT & ANGRES.	
	29/9/16		Horse transport heard ENE of Eastern end of BULLY Trench at 2 A.M. and 5 A.M. Rounds fired 750. Casualties NIL.	
	30/9/16	9.20 P.M. 10.00 P.M.	Guns shooting with 3 guns onto ROLLINCOURT CITE traversing between points M.21.c.71. M.27. B.2.5½. M.27. D.2.6½ M.26.D.5.2. 1500 Rounds. Casualties NIL.	

112th Brigade.
37th Division.

112th MACHINE GUN COMPANY

OCTOBER 1 9 1 6:

CONFIDENTIAL Vol 8

WAR DIARY
of
112 MACHINE GUN COY.

1st of October to 31st October 1916.

VOLUME VIII

[signature] O.C.
112 M. GUN COMPANY.

WAR DIARY or INTELLIGENCE SUMMARY

Army Form C. 2118.

VOL. VIII

[Signed] O.C. 112 M. GUN COMPANY

Place	Date	Hour	Summary of Events and Information	Remarks and references to Appendices
BULLY GRENAY	1.10.16		Casualties NIL. Work continued improving emplacements.	
	2/10/16		"	
	3/10/16		1 Gun moved from NADAUD to MORROW TRENCH. Extra emplacements constructed in MORROW. Rounds fired 3500 on targets as follows M.20.c.9.5 to M.27.c.12.7½, M.26.B.88, M.21.c.12½ to M.21.c.62. – DUMP at M.21.c.6. and CITÉ de ROLLINCOURT M.2.c.7.3	
	4.10.16		Casualties NIL. Rounds fired 1500 Target ROLLINCOURT M.26.B.88. M.21.c.12.1. M.21.c.62.– Trench tram emplacement in CARON D'AIX deepened and emplacement commenced. PYRENEES TRENCH deepened & new M.G. emplacement.	
	5.10.16		Casualties NIL. Work continued as on 4.10.16	
	6.10.16		Rounds fired 500 onto M.21.D.8.1. Work continued on above and Dugout commenced in PYRENEES. Casualties NIL.	
	7.10.16		Casualties NIL. Rounds fired 450 onto Crossroads M.21.d.8.1. Work carried on trench emplacements, revetting & dug-out boresting.	[signed] Sampling front

WAR DIARY or INTELLIGENCE SUMMARY.

Army Form C. 2118.

No. 12 M. GUN COMPANY.

Place	Date	Hour	Summary of Events and Information	Remarks and references to Appendices
BULLY GRENAY	8.10.16		Brigade front extended to CALONNE and 4 new emplacements were taken over by the Coy. from 111th M.G. Coy. 4 guns being moved into them.	
	9.10.16		Work proceeded on dugouts in PYRENEES emplacement & CAPDOPOINT. Casualties NIL. Guns moved from positions in ALGIERS to M.12.d.6.5.80. Work proceeded as before.	
	10.10.16		Rounds fired 1000 on Dumps at M.21.c.8.3. Work continued.	Daytime shots
	11.9.16		Work carried on as above. Rounds fired 1400 on M.27.B.2.5 & M.33.a.2.2.	
	12.10.16		Work continued in LEMCO TRENCH as above	
	13.10.16		2 Emplacements completed in MOROCCO SOUTH, other work continued	
	14.10.16		Work continued as above	
VERDREL	15.10.16		Company relieved by M.G. Coy 5th CAN Bde. Relief completed without incident at 12 n.r. Company marched to VERDREL billets.	
DIEVAL	16.10.16		Company proceeded to DIEVAL billets	
	17.10.16		Company rested at DIEVAL. 1 officer reinforcement.	Glen Neal

Army Form C. 2118.

WAR DIARY
or
INTELLIGENCE SUMMARY.
(Erase heading not required.)

No. 12 M/C GUN COMPANY.

Place	Date	Hour	Summary of Events and Information	Remarks and references to Appendices
FOUFFLIN-RICAMETZ	18/10/16		Company proceeded to billets in FOUFFLIN-RICAMETZ 2/Lt Lawrence transferred to Div. M.G.Coy as 2nd i/c Coy.	
	19/10/16		Company in Rest.	
PETIT BOURET	20/10/16		Company to new billets in PETIT BOURET. Office reinforcement.	
LONGUEVILETTE	21/10/16		Company proceeded to billets in LONGUEVILETTE	
SARTON	22/10/16		Company moved to SARTON. Major B.H. TUCKLE proceeded to M/G.T.C. GRANTHAM. Capt. G. GAUNTLETT reports and assumed command	
MAILLY-MAILLET	23/		Company proceeded to MAILLY-MAILLET and remains due in during the 29th Oct.	
ORVILLE	30/10/16		Company marches to ORVILLE to billets.	
DOULLENS	31/10/16		Company proceeds to DOULLENS to billets	

112th Brigade.
37th Division.

112th MACHINE GUN COMPANY

NOVEMBER 1 9 1 6:

Army Form C. 2118.

WAR DIARY
or
INTELLIGENCE SUMMARY.
(Erase heading not required.)

Vol IX

Instructions regarding War Diaries and Intelligence Summaries are contained in F.S. Regs., Part II. and the Staff Manual respectively. Title pages will be prepared in manuscript.

Stewart Capt.
O.C. 112 M. Gun Company.

Place	Date	Hour	Summary of Events and Information	Remarks and references to Appendices
DOULLENS	1.11.16 to 11.11.16		In rest billets. Training in preparation for future operations	Jno Stewart
VAUCHELLES	12.11.16		Moved to VAUCHELLES & stayed in billets one night	John Stewart
BERTRANCOURT	13.11.16		Moved to BERTRANCOURT & stayed in billets one night	John Stewart
MAILLY MAILLET	14.11.16		Moved to MAILLY-MAILLET & went into billets	John Stewart
	15.11.16	2 AM	Sections 3 & 4 moved up to WHITE CITY & took part in the attack on MUNICH TRENCH by the 112th Brigade	
		5 PM	Sections 1 & 2 moved up to WAGGON ROAD & BEAUMONT TRENCH & took over strong points from 13th K.R.R. & 2nd H.L.I. organising with 3 & 4 Sections a defensive zone of fire along the front & left flank of the Brigade. Casualties 1 OR Killed 5 OR Wounded	Jno Stewart
	16.11.16		Company held the same line. No attacks or counterattacks. Lieut. Picton AN wounded. Casualties 1 OR killed 5 OR Wounded	Jno Stewart

Vol IX

WAR DIARY
or
INTELLIGENCE SUMMARY.
(Erase heading not required.)

Army Form C. 2118.

No. 112 M. GUN COMPANY.

Place	Date	Hour	Summary of Events and Information	Remarks and references to Appendices
MAILLY MAILLET	17.11.16	6 AM	Company was relieved by the 96th M.G.Coy & returned to MAILLY-MAILLET	John Plummer Capt
ENGLEBELMER	18.11.16	3 PM	Moved to ENGLEBELMER & stayed in billets one night	John Plummer
	19.11.16		Moved to R23b 3.8. near HAMEL. Sections 1 & 2 moved up to STATION ROAD	John Plummer
			Casualties 108 Pte Mustart (wounded 16.11.16) died of wounds	
	19.11.16		No movement. Took place	John Plummer
	20.11.16		Sections 1 & 2 moved up to BEAUCOURT ROAD & took over from 111th M.G.Coy. Section #3 moved up to STATION ROAD R 11 d 4.5	John Plummer
			Casualties 1 O.R. wounded	
	21.11.16		Section 4 moved up to STATION ROAD R.12 C 00.	John Plummer
			Casualties 1 OR killed	
	22.11.16		Section 3 relieved Section 2 which returned to STATION ROAD	John Plummer
			Casualties 1 OR killed	
	23.11.16		Section 4 relieved Section 1 which returned to Station Road	John Plummer
		4.30 PM	Section 3 took part in an attack on the TRIANGLE R 6 c by	

WAR DIARY
or
INTELLIGENCE SUMMARY.
(Erase heading not required.)

Army Form C. 2118.

No. 112 M. GUN COMPANY.

Place	Date	Hour	Summary of Events and Information	Remarks and references to Appendices
ENGLEBELMER			10th L.N.L. supported by 2 Companies of the 6th Bedfords. Section 4 assisted the infantry with covering fire from the right flank. During this attack the infantry were held up by an enemy Machine Gun & Cpl Murrel & Pte Richardson distinguished themselves by bringing their gun into action, under intense fire, & silencing it, thereby allowing the infantry to proceed. Casualties 2 OR Killed 1 OR Wounded	John Stewart
	24.11.16		Section 2 relieved Section 3 which returned to STATION ROAD.	John Stewart
	25.11.16		The Company was relieved by the 91st M.G. Coy & returned to ENGLEBELMER staying there in billets for one night.	John Stewart
MAILLY-MAILLET	26.11.16		Moved to MAILLY-MAILLET & stayed there in billets for one night.	John Stewart
LOUVENCOURT	27.11.16		Moved to LOUVENCOURT & went into next billets	John Stewart
	28.11.16		Cleaned & inspected kit & equipment. Remained in rest billets. Training	John Stewart
RUBEMPRÉ	30.11.16		Moved to RUBEMPRÉ & went into billets	John Stewart

Vol IX

112th Brigade.
37th Division.

112th MACHINE GUN COMPANY

DECEMBER 1 9 1 6:

Army Form C. 2118.

WAR DIARY
or
INTELLIGENCE SUMMARY.
(Erase heading not required.)

[Signature] O.C.
No. 112 M. GUN COMPANY.

Instructions regarding War Diaries and Intelligence Summaries are contained in F.S. Regs., Part II. and the Staff Manual respectively. Title pages will be prepared in manuscript.

Place	Date	Hour	Summary of Events and Information	Remarks and references to Appendices
RUBEMPRE	1.12.16		Company in rest billets. General cleaning up.	Auf
"	2.12.16		Company training. Drill, mechanism. P.T. Lecture (Characteristics)	Auf
"	3.12.16		Church parade.	Auf
"	4.12.16		Company training. Squad drill. I.A. Visual training. P.T. Gun drill.	Auf
"	5.12.16		Company training. Company drill. Mechanism. P.T. Lecture (Indirect fire)	Auf
"	6.12.16		Company training. Range (Machine gun and revolver). P.T. Cleaning gun & lecture. (Range Card)	Auf
"	7.12.16		Company training. Kit inspection and I.A. Gun drill P.T. Spare parts.	Auf
"	8.12.16		Company training. Lectural scheme. Cleaning gun.	Auf
"	9.12.16		Company training. Company drill. Advanced gun drill. P.T. Lecture (map reading)	Auf
"	10.12.16		Church parade.	Auf
"	11.12.16		Company inspection by Brigadier. He expressed satisfaction at the smart appearance of the Company. Notification received that the Brigade might move at any moment.	Auf
"	12.12.16		Packing of limbers. Preparing to move.	Auf
"	13.12.16		Left RUBEMPRE at 9 a.m. Arrived BEAUVAL 2 p.m. Distance covered 8½ MILES.	Auf
BEAUVAL	14.12.16		Left BEAUVAL at 8.30 a.m. Arrived VILLIER LE HÔPITAL 5.0 p.m. Distance covered 14½ miles.	Auf

WAR DIARY or INTELLIGENCE SUMMARY

Army Form C. 2118.

112 M. GUN COMPANY.

Place	Date	Hour	Summary of Events and Information	Remarks and references to Appendices
VILLIER LE HOPITAL	15.12.16		Left Villier le Hopital at 10 a.m. Arrived Blangermont 1.30 p.m. Distance covered 9 miles.	
BLANGEMONT	16.12.16		Left Blangemont at 8.15 a.m. Arrived Anvin 1 p.m. Distance covered 10 miles.	
ANVIN	17.12.16		Left Anvin at 4.30 a.m. Arrived Bellery 12.20 p.m. Distance covered 10 miles.	
BELLERY	18.12.16		Left Bellery at 9 a.m. Arrived Laleau 1.30 p.m. Distance covered 9 miles.	
LALEAU	19.12.16		Prepared guns etc. for line. Overhauled spare parts.	
LALEAU	20.12.16		Left Laleau 9 a.m. Arrived Le Touret 1.45 p.m. Distance covered 10 miles.	
SLOANE SQUARE	21.12.16		Company housed in billets at Sloane Square. Issued clothing and completed three sections for the line.	
	22.12.16		Three groups (consisting of three guns each) under the command of 2 Lt. Thurnick h.1. Montp, 2nd Lt. Palmer h.2 grop, and Lt. Pemmen h.3 grop, left B.H.Q. at 5 a.m. for the trenches, to relieve part of 15th Machine Gun Coy. The H grop (consisting of three guns) left B.H.Q. at 8 a.m. for the trenches to relieve part of 95th Machine Gun Coy. Both relief were completed at 10 a.m. without any hitch.	
		3.30 p.m	A number in shifts applied on h.5 gun emplacement of h.1 grop, and destroyed the gun, limber, and all spare parts. The trench (Cover Trench) was	

WAR DIARY
or
INTELLIGENCE SUMMARY.

(Erase heading not required.)

Army Form C. 2118.

No. 2 M. GUN COMPANY

Place	Date	Hour	Summary of Events and Information	Remarks and references to Appendices
SLOANE SQUARE	23.12.16		Very much damaged. No casualties to gun team.	
			The firing line carried on by the Company. A great deal of work was done improving emplacements, dug outs and trenches between	
		4 p.m.	a minimum to shell distances. No 5 gun emplacement, the gun being rendered unfit. No casualties occurred.	
SLOANE SQUARE	24.12.16	12.0.m.	Indirect fire was carried out by this Company at 8.1 mm on the following table.	
SLOANE SQUARE	25.12.16	8 a.m.		

POSITION OF GUN	TARGET	ROUNDS FIRED	RESULT
HAYSTACK POST.	Communication trench at S22D S28B S23C	5250	Unknown
	S29 A		
ORCHARD POST	DISTILLERY S19 CENTRAL	2000	Unknown
	CROSS TRAMWAYS S23 a 2.3	4000	Unknown
DOGS POST	CROSS ROADS S23 LA	4000	Unknown
	TOURELLE S.19 A 8.5, 6.		
OATS POST	CROSS ROADS S23 B 5.5.3.	1,400	Unknown

TOTAL ROUNDS FIRED 19,060

MAP REF.
RICHBOURG
Sheet 36 S.W. 3.

Army Form C. 2118.

WAR DIARY
or
INTELLIGENCE SUMMARY.
(Erase heading not required.)

No. 12 [?] COMPANY.

Place	Date	Hour	Summary of Events and Information	Remarks and references to Appendices
			Two new indirect fire emplacements were constructed, and dug outs put in order.	
			Two gun teams on den 2nd lt [?] Mc Graw, and 2nd lt. L.R.B Woolford left	
	25.12.16	9.a.m	R.H.Q at 9 a.m. for the trenches to carry out indirect fire during	
			the Christmas "strafe". They were joined by three guns from Haystack	
			trenches, i.e. nos 1, 2, 3, and 4 guns.	
SLOANE SQUARE	25.12.16	8 a.m	Indirect fire were carried out by this company as shown by the following table.	
	to	to		
	26.12.16	9.a.m		

POSITION OF GUN	TARGET	ROUNDS FIRED	RESULT
HAYSTACK POST.	Communication trenches at S22d S28b S23c S29a.	13,000	Unknown
ORCHARD POST.	CROSS TRAMWAYS S22 a. 2,3.	18,000	Unknown
	DISTILLERY S.M.[?]	9,000	Unknown
DOGS POST.	CROSS ROADS LA TOURELLE		
	S.M a.8.6.	10,000	Unknown
CATS POST.	CROSS ROADS S23 b9,3	2,500	Unknown
	TOTAL ROUNDS FIRED	52,500	

MAP REF.
RICHEBOURG
Sheet 36 SW 3

WAR DIARY or INTELLIGENCE SUMMARY

Army Form C. 2118.

No. 2 M.G. GUN COMPANY

Place	Date	Hour	Summary of Events and Information	Remarks and references to Appendices
SLOANE SQUARE	23.12.16	8 a.m.	Intermittent and retaliatory fire continued.	
	24.12.16	8 a.m.	The following indirect fire was carried out by this Company on 23rd and 24th inst. night 23rd/24th inst.	

POSITION OF GUN	TARGET	ROUNDS FIRED	RESULT
HAYSTACK POST 3 GUNS	Communication trenches at S.28d S.23c S.29a	42,000	Unknown
ORCHARD POST 3 GUNS	Cross Tramways S.23.a. 23. Communication trenches and strong points at S.14.a.1.5. & a. S.14.b.4, S.23.a.4,8.b. S.23.b.1-4	33,000	Unknown
DOGS POST 3 GUNS	DISTILLERY S.14 CENTRAL CROSS ROADS S.14.a.8.5,b. " S.23.b.9.3.	7,000 10,000 10,000	Unknown Unknown Unknown

TOTAL ROUNDS FIRED 102,000

MAP REF.,
RICHEBOURG.
Sheet 36 S.W.3

WAR DIARY
or
INTELLIGENCE SUMMARY

(Erase heading not required.)

Army Form C. 2118.

No. 12 M. GUN COMPANY.

Place	Date	Hour	Summary of Events and Information	Remarks and references to Appendices
			This concluded our Christmas shoot in conjunction with the Artillery and Trench Mortar batteries. The object of the shoot was quite successful, the Enemy making no attempt to fraternise.	
SLOANE SQUARE	27.12.16	8 a.m.	The firing was done by the Company during the 24 hours owing to the	
	28.12.16	8 a.m.	reorganisation of the Machine Gun Defence Scheme, the existing positions of guns being found unsuitably imposible. Eleven positions being practically finalised with one gun in reserve. This was allotted to four guns in front line, four guns in support and four guns in reserve, forming Belts of fire across the respective fronts, the Four Guns in reserve and of the four guns in support can carry out indirect fire.	Cat.
SLOANE SQUARE	28.12.16	8 a.m.	The following indirect fire was carried out by this Company	
	29.12.16	8 a.m.		Cat.

POSITION	TARGET	ROUNDS FIRED	RESULT	MAP REF.
DOGS POST	S14 a 8.6	450	Unknown	RICHEBOURGH
ORCHARD POST	SM a 1.4.6 / S14 a 9.4	1000	Unknown	Sheet 36 SW 5

TOTAL ROUNDS FIRED 1450

Army Form C. 2118.

WAR DIARY
or
INTELLIGENCE SUMMARY.
(Erase heading not required.)

No. N2 M. GUN COMPANY

Place	Date	Hour	Summary of Events and Information	Remarks and references to Appendices
			Work done: — Alternative Emplacements were started in all positions. Dug outs strengthened. The Brigadier fully approved of new scheme, and after inspecting all gun positions, was satisfied that the belts of fire could not be improved on.	
SLOANE SQUARE	29.12.16	8.a.m.	Indirect fire was carried out by this Company as shown in the following table.	
	30.12.16	8.a.m.		

POSITION OF GUN	TARGET	ROUNDS FIRED	TIME	RESULT	MAP REF.
DEAD COW POST	ROAD junction to TRAMWAY S23b 9.3 to S23.C.h.3.	2000	10.30 p.m. to 1.0 a.m.	Unknown	RICHEBOURG Sheet 36.S.W.3
DOGS POST	CROSS ROADS LA TOURELLE S14a&m	2000	6p.m. to 9.0p.m. 10.0 p.m to 1 a.m	Unknown	
ORCHARD POST	Communication trenche S14a15.m S14a 6.4 S23a.Y.6 S23b1.Y	2000	8.30 p.m. to 11.30 p.m	Unknown	

TOTAL ROUNDS FIRED 6000

WAR DIARY or INTELLIGENCE SUMMARY.

Army Form C. 2118.

112 M. Gun Company

(Erase heading not required.)

Place	Date	Hour	Summary of Events and Information	Remarks and references to Appendices
Sloane Square	30.12.16	6 a.m.	Work done. Eight new emplacements built.	[signature]
	31.12.16	12 M.	Harrassing fire was carried out as usual as shown by the following table.	

Position of Gun.	Target.	Rounds Fired	Time.	Result.
Dogs Post.	S14.a.8.4.	6000	4-8 p.m. 9-11 p.m. 6-8 a.m.	Unknown
Orchard Post.	Searching fire with 6° traverse on Tramway & Cross Rds. S25.b.4.3. S25.c.9.3.	2000	10:30 p.m. 12 M. 5-6 a.m. 7-30 a.m.	Unknown
Dead Cow Post. 2 Guns.	Cross Tramways. S23.a.2.5.	2000	9.p.m. 12 M. 6-9 a.m.	Unknown
	Cross Roads S29.a. 6.4.5.0.	1000	9-10 p.m.	Unknown
Total Rounds Fired	11000			

Map Ref.
Richebourg
Sheet 36 S.W. 3.

[signature]

Secret

WAR of DIARY Vol XI

112 MACHINE GUN COY

1st of January to 31st of January 1917

(Volume XI)

Army Form C. 2118.

WAR DIARY
or
INTELLIGENCE SUMMARY
(Erase heading not required.)

Army Form No. XI

S. Gun Sun Capt.
15 Machine Gun Coy

Place	Date	Hour	Summary of Events and Information				Remarks and references to Appendices
SLOANE SQUARE	1-1-19	12.16m to	Indirect fire was carried out by the Company as shown in the following table				
	2-1-19	8.a.m.	POSITION OF GUN	TARGET	ROUNDS FIRED	TIME	RESULT
			3 C	Searching trenches on Communication trenches at S.23.a.22.5	2000	12 a.m. 4.30 p.m.	Unknown
			4 C	Junction of trenches and STRONG POINT S.16.D.8.45	5500	12 a.m. 4 a.m.	Unknown	MAP REF. RICHEBOURG 10,000 36 S.W.3
			1 B	Road and adjoining trenches from S.29.b.5.4.5 to S.29.a.4-6. Junction of roads at S.29.d.4.4	2500	12 a.m. 4 a.m.	Unknown
				TOTAL ROUNDS FIRED	9 000		
SLOANE SQUARE	2-1-19	8 a.m. to	The Allowing indirect fire was carried out.				
	3-1-19	8 a.m.	POSITION OF GUN	TARGET	ROUNDS FIRED	TIME	RESULT
			HAYSTACK POST	Junction of roads at S.14.a.9.5.6.	1500	6.10 p.m.	Unknown
			ORCHARD POST	Communication from m TRENCHES from S.23.a.6.6 to S.23.4.0	2600	4 p.m. 12 Midnight	Unknown

Army Form C. 2118.

WAR DIARY
or
INTELLIGENCE SUMMARY.
(Erase heading not required.)

Instructions regarding War Diaries and Intelligence Summaries are contained in F. S. Regs., Part II. and the Staff Manual respectively. Title pages will be prepared in manuscript.

Place	Date	Hour	Summary of Events and Information	Remarks and references to Appendices
SLOANE SQUARE				
			POSITION OF GUN / TARGET / ROUNDS FIRED / TIME / RESULT / MAP REF.	
			DOGS POST / Junction of TRENCHES at S16d 8,4,5. / 2000 / 4.30 p.m to 9 p.m / Unknown / RICHEBOURG. 1/10,000 36 S.W. 3	
			TOTAL ROUNDS FIRED. 5500.	
			Work done. Light new emplacements and medical Ammunition shelters started and dug out strengthened. Indirect fire was carried out at under.	Aust
SLOANE SQUARE	5·1·17	8 a.m		
	4·1·17	9 a.m	POSITION OF GUN / TARGET / ROUNDS FIRED / RESULT / TIME / MAP REF.	
			DOGS POST. / Junction of ROAD and PATH at S11c 2,8. / 1500. / Unknown / 6 p.m to 8 p.m / RICHEBOURG. 1/10,000 36 S.W. 3	
			ORCHARD POST. / MITZI TRENCH showered from / 1500 / Unknown / 6 p.m to 10 p.m	
			S11 c 5,3 to S11 c 4,2.	
			3B. / PIANO HOUSE S24 c 4.0 / 2000 / Unknown / 4 p.m to 6 a.m	
			O.B.L. / RUE DU MARAIS S29 a 9,4. / 2000 / Unknown / 6 p.m to 12 M.	
			TOTAL ROUNDS FIRED. 4000	

WAR DIARY
or
INTELLIGENCE SUMMARY.
(Erase heading not required.)

Army Form C. 2118.

Place	Date	Hour	Summary of Events and Information				Remarks and references to Appendices
SLOANE SQUARE	4/1/19	8 a.m.	Work done. Work was carried on with the emplacements and a dug out started at A.I. position. Ammunition was dumped at the new positions.				Ainsf
	5/1/19	8 a.m.	harassing fire was carried out at under.				
			Position of Gun	Target	Rounds Fired	Time	Result
			O.B.L.	Rue du Marais S29 a 9.4	2000	6.30 p.m.	Unknown
			B2a	Fme. de Toulotte S22 b 8.6.	3000	10.30 p.m. 5.30 p.m. 11.30 p.m.	Unknown
			Dogs Post.	La Tourelle x Rds. S14 a 8.4.	2000	6.15 p.m. 11.30 p.m.	Unknown
			Orchard Post.	x Tramways S14 a 5.5	1000	7 p.m. 12 M	Unknown
				Total Rounds Fired 8000.			Map Ref. Richebourg. Sheet 36 S.W. 3. 1/10,000.
SLOANE SQUARE	5/1/19	8 a.m.	A great deal of work was done on indirect fire emplacements, and new dug outs.				Ainsf
	6/1/19	8 a.m.	The following harassing fire was carried out.				
			Position of Gun	Target	Rounds Fired	Time	Result
			O.B.L.	Rue du Marais S29 a 9.4	2000	2 a.m. 6 a.m.	Unknown
			Dogs Post	La Tourelle x Rds. S14 a 8.4	2000	2 a.m. 6 a.m.	Unknown
			B3o.	C.T.S. S25 b 3.4. S23 b 9.3.	2000	2 a.m. 6 a.m.	Unknown
				Total Rounds Fired 8000.			Map Ref. Richebourg. Sheet 36 S.W. 3. 1/10,000.

WAR DIARY
or
INTELLIGENCE SUMMARY

Army Form C. 2118.

(Erase heading not required.)

Instructions regarding War Diaries and Intelligence Summaries are contained in F. S. Regs., Part II. and the Staff Manual respectively. Title pages will be prepared in manuscript.

Place	Date	Hour	Summary of Events and Information	Remarks and references to Appendices
SLOANE SQUARE	6-1-16	8 a.m.	Indirect fire was carried out as shown on the following table.	
	7-1-16	2 a.m.		

Table 1:

POSITION OF GUN	TARGET	ROUNDS FIRED	HOURS	RESULT	MAP REF.
DOGS POST.	LA TOURELLE x RDS. S.14 a 8.9	2000	2 a.m. 6 a.m.	Unknown	RICHEBOURG Sheet 36 S.W.3 1/10,000
ORCHARD POST.	CROSS TRAMWAYS. S.14 a 3.5.	2000	2 a.m. 6 a.m.	"	"
3B	RUE DE MARAIS. S.29 b 0.4.	2000	2 a.m. 6 a.m.	"	"

TOTAL ROUNDS FIRED. 6000

We connected up an O.P. with two indirect fire guns by telephone to that parties of Germans can be fired on by indirect fire with observation, the guns being laid on ROADS the men frequently use.

			Indirect fire was carried out as follows.	
SLOANE SQUARE	7-1-16	6 a.m.		
	8-1-16	9 a.m.		

Table 2:

POSITION OF GUN	TARGET	ROUNDS FIRED	TIME	RESULT	MAP REF.
ORCHARD POST.	TRENCHES W. of LA TOURELLE S.14 a 3.5.	2000	9 p.m. 3 a.m. 6 a.m.	Unknown	RICHEBOURG Sheet 36 S.W.3 1/10,000
DOGS POST.	LA TOURELLE x RDS. S.14 a 8.9.	2000	2 a.m. 6.30 a.m.	Unknown	"

TOTAL ROUNDS FIRED. 4000

WAR DIARY
or
INTELLIGENCE SUMMARY.
(Erase heading not required.)

Army Form C. 2118.

Place	Date	Hour	Summary of Events and Information	Remarks and references to Appendices
SLOANE SQUARE.	8/1/16	8 a.m.	Indented for emplacements for Light mortar guns were started and platform fixed.	
	9/1/16	9 a.m.	The following indirect fire was carried out:	

POSITION OF GUN	TARGET	ROUNDS FIRED	TIME	RESULT	MAP REF.
DOGS POST.	Junction of Trench and Road S.11.C.3.5.3	1600	2 a.m. 6 a.m.	Unknown	RICHEBOURG. Sheet 36 S.W.3
B.3.	Rue du Marais S.29.b.0.4.	500	5 a.m. 6 a.m.	"	1/10,000

TOTAL ROUNDS FIRED 1500.

Temporary emplacements were erected in anticipation for the straffe on the morning of the 10th. A big indirect fire "shoot" was carried out by the company with the artillery and french mortars. Details as follows:

POSITION OF GUNS	TARGET	ROUNDS FIRED	TIME	RESULT
SLOANE SQUARE 9/1/16 8 a.m. HAYSTACK POST.	ENEMY TRENCHES S.16.b.1.5. to S.16.b.6.9. and 5° each side. S.16.b.3.5.9.6.			
10/1/16 6.30 a.m. 4 GUNS	to S.16.b.0.5.0.3. and 5° each side S.16.a.1.6. to S.16.a.2.2. and 5° each side.			

Army Form C. 2118.

WAR DIARY
or
INTELLIGENCE SUMMARY.
(Erase heading not required.)

Instructions regarding War Diaries and Intelligence Summaries are contained in F.S. Regs., Part II. and the Staff Manual respectively. Title pages will be prepared in manuscript.

Place	Date	Hour	Summary of Events and Information	Remarks and references to Appendices
			POSITION OF GUN — TARGET — ROUNDS FIRED — TIME — RESULT	
			HAYSTACK POST — Enemy Trenches S16 b 5.6, 0.5 to S16 a 9.3, 0.3 and 50 each side — 14,600 — 4 a.m. to 8.30 a.m. — Undistinct	
			DOGS POST 3 GUNS — Enemy Trenches. S22 Central — 8,000 — 4 a.m. 8.30 a.m. — "	MAP REF. RICHEBOURG Sheet 36.S.W.3.
			EDWARDS POST 3 GUNS — Enemy Trenches S22.a.b.c.d — 12,625 — 4 a.m. 8.30 a.m.	
			LANSDOWNE POST 3 GUNS — Enemy Front and Support Lines S16 a and b. — 16,860 — 4 a.m. 8.30 a.m. — "	
			ORCHARD POST 3 GUNS — Communication Trenches S22.a — 10,000 — 4 a.m. 8.30 a.m. — "	/10,000.
			TOTAL ROUNDS FIRED 61,445.	

Great damage must have been done as the Enemy bombarded very heavily and searched for all our gun positions many having escapes and Dogs Post blown in. The guns and teams had been withdrawn, luckily as the position received a great many direct hits.

WAR DIARY
or
INTELLIGENCE SUMMARY.

Army Form C. 2118.

(Erase heading not required.)

Place	Date	Hour	Summary of Events and Information	Remarks and references to Appendices
SLOANE SQUARE	10/1/14	8.30am	Our machine guns did not fire owing to the	
	11/1/14	8 am	original positions, the drying and overhauling of guns and spare parts. Dogs Post was cleaned and built to replace it. Enemy Artillery again worked for an emplacement without success.	Cwf
SLOANE SQUARE	11/1/14	8 am	Indirect fire was carried out as follows.	

	POSITION OF GUN.	TARGET.	ROUNDS FIRED.	RESULT.	TIME	MAP REF.
	B2.	RUE DU MARAIS. S29a 9.3.	2500.	Unknown	5 a.m. 6.30 a.m	RICHEBOURG. 36 S.W.3.

| | 12/1/14 | 8 am | Lewis guns were fitted in to strengthen our scheme of defence and the positions were observed (suggested by Capt. Gauntlett) by the Brigadier and the Battalion L.O.a. | Cwf |
| SLOANE SQUARE | 13/1/14 | 8 am | While guns negotiated on S.Md 5.5.O.D. there was no firing was done. Observation was very difficult owing to inpenetrable weather conditions. All morning in No.2 Platoon were checked with the aid of the Divisional Bombard, and range cards altered. All small Box respirators were tested and found in good condition. | Cwf |

Army Form C. 2118.

WAR DIARY
or
INTELLIGENCE SUMMARY.
(Erase heading not required.)

Instructions regarding War Diaries and Intelligence Summaries are contained in F.S. Regs., Part II. and the Staff Manual respectively. Title pages will be prepared in manuscript.

Place	Date	Hour	Summary of Events and Information	Remarks and references to Appendices
SLOANE SQUARE.	13/1/19	8 a.m.	Indirect fire was carried out by this Company at Amalin. Map Ref.	
	14/1/19	8 a.m.	POSITION OF GUN — TARGET — ROUNDS FIRED — TIME — RESULT — RICHEBOURG. 36 S.W.3	
			B1. — RUE DU MARAIS S29 a 9.3. — 3000 — 2 a.m. 7 a.m. — Unknown	
			Our wire guns did not fire owing to a heavy mist. New T pieces & through rifle were fixed into indirect fire emplacements.	Arb. J.
SLOANE SQUARE	14/1/19	8 a.m.	No firing was done and the weather was too bad for observation. Work was again carried out on emplacements dug outs and trenches.	Arb. J.
SLOANE SQUARE	15/1/19	8.0 a.m.	Our guns did not fire during the twenty four hours. On anti-aircraft mounting	
	16/1/19	8 a.m.	gun placed in position and a drum instructor has to repel hostile aircraft. Shelters were made water tight to store ammunition.	Arb. J.
SLOANE SQUARE.	16/1/19	8 a.m.	Indirect fire was carried out as shown on the following table.	
	17/1/19	8 a.m.	POSITION OF GUN — TARGET — ROUNDS FIRED — TIME — RESULT — MAP REF.	
			BREWERY POST. — ADALBERT ALLEY S22d 4.5.3 to S23 — 1900 — 3 p.m. — Unknown — RICHEBOURG 36 S.W.3
			C.1.2.				6.15 p.m.	"	
			ORCHARD POST. — C.T. S22 d1.4 to S22.3.5. — 1960 — 3 p.m., 3.20 p.m. — " — "
			Do. — C.T. S22 b.5.1 to S22 b.6.2 — 2450 — 3 p.m., 3.20 p.m. — " — "

Army Form C. 2118.

WAR DIARY
or
INTELLIGENCE SUMMARY.
(Erase heading not required.)

Instructions regarding War Diaries and Intelligence Summaries are contained in F.S. Regs., Part II. and the Staff Manual respectively. Title pages will be prepared in manuscript.

Place	Date	Hour	Summary of Events and Information	Remarks and references to Appendices
			POSITION OF GUN. — **TARGET.** — **ROUNDS FIRED** — **TIME** — **RESULT.**	
			HAYSTACK POST. — ADALBERT ALLEY S22 0.4 to S22 d.5.2.6. — 2060 — 3 p.m. / 4 p.m. — Unknown	
			TOTAL ROUNDS FIRED. 8300	
			The usual work was carried out on emplacements and dug-outs, more T pieces being fitted in to modernise emplacements. Owing to the weather observation was impossible from O.P. Indirect fire was carried out as usual.	
SLOANE SQUARE	19.1.19	8 a.m.	**POSITION OF GUN.** — **TARGET.** — **ROUNDS FIRED** — **TIME** — **RESULT.** — **MAP REF.**	
			ORCHARD POST. — CROSS TRAMWAYS S23 a 2.2. — — 12 M. to 6.30 a.m. — Unknown — RICHEBOURG 36 S.W.3.	
			2 GUNS. — MITZI C.T. S11 C 33 to S11 C 4.2. — 5250 — 6.30 a.m. — Unknown	
			DEAD COW. — C.T. S23 b 2.3 to S23 b 8.3. —	
			3 GUNS. — PIANO HOUSE S24 C W.0 0.5 — — 12 M. to 6.30 a.m. — Unknown	
			RUE DE MARAIS. S29 a 0.0 4.5 to S29 b 4.0 5.3. — 3000	
			TOTAL ROUNDS FIRED. 6250.	

WAR DIARY or INTELLIGENCE SUMMARY

Army Form C. 2118.

Place	Date	Hour	Summary of Events and Information	Remarks and references to Appendices
SLOANE SQUARE	18.1.19	8 am	Work was carried out at wheel and a new timber post in to strengthen existing woodwork in dug outs and emplacements. Low visibility again prevented the wire gun from firing.	
	19.1.19	9 am	The following indirect fire was carried out by MG Company.	

POSITION OF GUN	TARGET	ROUNDS FIRED	TIME	RESULT
DOGS POST	C.T. S22 b 0.5 to S22 d 6.9	3000	1·50 pm / 2·30 pm	Unknown
EDWARD POST	Junction of Quinque Rue and Nora Trench. S14 c 0.0.5.5.	500	2 pm / 2·30 pm	"
ORCHARD POST	Adalbert Alley S22 d 6.0.3.5 to S25 c 3.1.	2000	1 pm / 2 pm	"
	Eitel Alley S28 b 5.8. to S29 a 2.6.	2250	1 pm / 2·30 pm	"
PALL MALL	X Roads at S25 b 8.5.3.0.	345	1·45 pm / 2 pm	"
B 2	C.T. S25 a 0.1. to S25 a 4.5.4.5.	1800	1·15 pm / 1·30	"
	TOTAL ROUNDS FIRED	9,925		

Army Form C. 2118.

WAR DIARY
or
INTELLIGENCE SUMMARY.
(Erase heading not required.)

Instructions regarding War Diaries and Intelligence Summaries are contained in F.S. Regs., Part II. and the Staff Manual respectively. Title pages will be prepared in manuscript.

Place	Date	Hour	Summary of Events and Information	Remarks and references to Appendices
SLOANE Square	19/11/17	6.0am	From PALL MALL position S15b 45 75 m.c guns were employed between the hours of 1.0 & 4-0 pm. At 1.15 pm a party of 40 Germans were seen on road S30a 05 49 (from O.P.) The gun was brought into the target & 500 rounds were fired with successful results. At 1.40 pm fire was opened from same position on a party of 6 Germans in Field S17b 53 approximately - result successful - one man was hit & rest dispersed hurried. 500 rounds fired - German observed left of "CAMON FLAGHE" in field close to tree. Fire opened and man disappeared - 100 rounds fired. At 3.30 pm two of the enemy were observed in field behind "CAMOUFAGHE" tree moving south - fire was opened but owing to bad light result could not be observed. The following indirect fire was carried out	[signature]
	20/11/17	6.0am		

Position	Target	Rounds fired	Hrs	Result
S21b 05 60	Tramway & Road junction S23 b 40 35 & S23 b 9.4	2000	4.0 pm to 8.30 pm	unknown
Dogs Post	S17a 8 60 LA TOURELLE Cross Roads	1000	4.30 pm to 6.30 pm	"
1B	RUE DE MARAIS	2006	5.0 pm to 9.0 pm	"

T2134. Wt. W708—776. 500000. 4/15. Sir J. C. & S.

Army Form C. 2118.

WAR DIARY
or
INTELLIGENCE SUMMARY.
(Erase heading not required.)

Instructions regarding War Diaries and Intelligence Summaries are contained in F.S. Regs., Part II. and the Staff Manual respectively. Title pages will be prepared in manuscript.

Place	Date	Hour	Summary of Events and Information	Remarks and references to Appendices
SLOANE SQUARE	19/11/17	8.0 AM	Hostile Offensive - Artillery searched along O.B.L. for our position but without success - our teams having to be withdrawn.	
	20/11/17	8.0 AM	Intelligence - Observation fair - enemy moving freely behind lines - enemy opposite to us QUINQUE RUE from LA TOURELLE to NORA TRENCH, in daylight for small working parties.	EB
SLOANE SQUARE	20/11/17	8.0 AM	Our Offensive - 250 rounds fired by our guns at 2 Germans walking along QUINQUE RUE S17c31 to S17c16 at 1.15 pm - enemy ducked & jumped fell into ditch. At 2.15 pm fire opened on a German in trench at S17c45. At 3.0 pm we fired at a German at S17d4035 - result unobserved. Indirect fire carried out as follows	
	21/11/17	8.0 AM		

Position	Target	Rds Fired	Hrs Fired	Result
DOGS POST 1.B	Junction of Path & Road. S17c2.8.	1500	5.30 & 8.30 pm	Unknown
	RUE de MARAIS & EITEL ALLEY S29a83 to S29b.1.4	2500	6.00 & 8.00 pm 3.0 to 5.0 am	?

Intelligence - Observation maintained from FACTORY O.P. during daylight

WAR DIARY
or
INTELLIGENCE SUMMARY
(Erase heading not required.)

Army Form C. 2118.

Place	Date	Hour	Summary of Events and Information	Remarks and references to Appendices
SLOANE SQUARE	21/4/17	8·0 am	The use of QUINQUE RUE north of NORA TRENCH by enemy confirmed. A German was observed about 1·0 p.m. in enemy front line at S.16.5.8. A hostile battery was observed firing from approximately S.29.b.5.0.	C.O. [signature]
	22/4/17	8·0 am	Our Offensive - Indirect fire with observation carried out	

Position	Target	Rds fired	Time	Result
PALL MALL	German ??? trench MORA C.T. S.23.b.33	40	11.15 AM	man jumped into trench. No further targets were observed
do	came target alone to obtain observation	50	11.30 a.m.	unobserved
do	slight movement observed on ??? point S.17.d.40.35	50	12.00 noon	do
do	Dugouts fm in PIONEER DUMP S.23.b.63	50	12.30 p.m.	do
do	Gun flash seen just N of F^{me} de TOULETTE S.22.b.7.5.0 - fire opened up barrage to left for ranging a roof of farm building	215	2.15 p.m.	H/gets MG replied with 5 rounds at once
do	faint movement observed near M building of DISTILLERY	110	2.30	unobserved

WAR DIARY or INTELLIGENCE SUMMARY

Army Form C. 2118.

Place	Date	Hour	Summary of Events and Information				Remarks and references to Appendices
			(cont'd)				
			Position	Target	Rds fired	Time	Result
			ORCHARD	ADALBERT ALLEY S20D44 S20D82	1756	6pm 7pm 4.30am 6.0am	Unknown
			DOGS	LA TOURELLE CROSS ROADS S17A 8560	1750	6.30 to 7.30 pm 5.30 to 6.30 am	do
			I.B.	CROSS ROADS S29D4075 Brick field S29D79	2000	7. t59 pm 2. t5 am	do
		Our offensive Artillery	Indirect fire and Observation				
			Position	Target	Rds fired	Time	Result
SLOANE SQUARE	22/11/17 8.0am to 23/11/17 8.0am		PALL MALL	Germans in field behind CAMOUFLAGE tree	25	10.55 am	Accurate finish
			do	2 Germans in field left of DISTILLERY	20	11.30 am	Unknown
			do	6 " " right of PIANO HOUSE	50	11.45 "	Party scattered
			do	2 " " in tramway about S23C88	30	12.45 pm	- dispersed
			do	3 " " in field left of PIANO House	30	12.45 "	- hit
			do	1 - S17d 10 45 (gun stand fire under urgent) men	35	3.30 "	man hit

Army Form C. 2118.

WAR DIARY
or
INTELLIGENCE SUMMARY.
(Erase heading not required.)

Instructions regarding War Diaries and Intelligence Summaries are contained in F.S. Regs., Part II. and the Staff Manual respectively. Title pages will be prepared in manuscript.

Place	Date	Hour	Summary of Events and Information					Remarks and references to Appendices
			Position	Target	Rounds	Time	Result	
			ORCHARD	ADALBERT ALLEY S20d44 to S20d82	1500	5.30 to 9.0 pm	Unobserved	
			DOGS	NORA TRENCH S16d 8075	2000	5 to 6 pm / 9.30 to 10.30 pm	do	
			1 B	RUE de MARAIS S26b23 to S29A7055	2000	5.30 to 9.0 pm	do	C.B.
			Enemy Offensive very quiet. Indirect fire carried out by us.					
SLOANE SQUARE	23/11/17 8.0am to 24/11/17 8.0am		Position	Target	Rounds	Time	Result	
			3 C	ADALBERT ALLEY S20d44 to S20d82	2000	5.30 to 6.30 pm / 6.0 am to 7.0 am	Unknown	
			DOGS	NORA TRENCH S16d 8075	2000	5.30 to 6.30 pm / 5.30 to 6.30 am	do	
			1 B	RUE de MARAIS S28B33 to S29A7055	2000	5.30 to 9.0 pm	do	
			S20b6684 / S21C1333	S29A 6560	3000	8.0 pm to 2.0 am	do	
			Enemy Offensive very quiet. Intelligence 2 Germans gave themselves up at BOARS HEAD at 9.0 pm					C.B.
			Hostile Indirect fire carried out by us.					
			Position	Target	Rounds	Time	Result	
SLOANE SQUARE	24/11/17 8.0am to 25/11/17 8.0am		DOGS	NORA TRENCH S16d 8075	2000	6.30 to 7.0 pm / 5.30 to 6.30 pm	Unknown	

T2134. Wt. W708-776. 500000. 4/15. Sir J. C. & S.

WAR DIARY
or
INTELLIGENCE SUMMARY.
(Erase heading not required.)

Army Form C. 2118.

Place	Date	Hour	Summary of Events and Information				Remarks and references to Appendices
			Position	Target	Rounds	Time	Result
			3 C	ADALBERT ALLEY S20d 44 to S20d 82	2000	5.30 to 6.30 am / 6.0 pm to 9.30 pm	Unknown
			1 B	RUE de MARAIS S29A 2550 to S29A 6560	2000	7.0 pm to 11.30 pm	do
			HAYSTACK S29A 6560		2000	7.0 pm to 11.30 pm	do C.B.
			Hostile Offensive - Very quiet				
SLOANE SQUARE	25/11/17 8.0 am to 26/11/17 8.0 pm		Our Offensive - We fired on S.23.d from 9.45 pm to 12.0 midnight in cooperation with Artillery who shelled German line N & S of FERME COUR d'Avoué. Rounds fired = " " " " 1125. Hostile Offensive - Shelled our front line support in vicinity of ROPE C.T. from 3.30 to 4.30 pm. Intelligence - O.P. not used owing to large amount of work in heavy C.O.				
SLOANE SQUARE	26/11/17 8.0 am to 27/11/17 8.0 am		Our Offensive - Our guns fired all night on S.23.A.B. 3000 rounds ADALBERT ALLEY 3500 rounds S20d 44 to S20d 62 MITZI C.T. & buildings S11C 735 S11C 72 - 7500 rounds NORA C.T. and road S16D 8075, S29 Rds S7C 0055, Rue de MARAIS S29A 25 to S29A 76 4000 rounds. Our 18 pounders shelled heavily at 10.0 pm. Hostile Offensive - Shelled ourselves route S of CADBURY C.T. 11.15 pm and dropped C.O. 5.9's in vicinity of DEAD COW POST				

WAR DIARY
or
INTELLIGENCE SUMMARY.
(Erase heading not required.)

Army Form C. 2118.

Place	Date	Hour	Summary of Events and Information	Remarks and references to Appendices
SLOANE SQUARE	27/11/17 to 28/11/17	5.0am to 8.0am	Our offensive — Organised fire of our M.G.s — 4 guns fired from front line into hostile front line N15a of COUR d'AVOUE, harassing the flanks of the raiding party and taking an hostile M.G. (1 Lewis M.G. was silenced by one of our guns (at S22a70) A barrage around the hostile sector was formed by the other 12 guns of the company which fired continuously during the whole of the raid. 1000 rounds expended. Hostile offensive. T.M. bombs were dropped during the raid on our front line att's and of ROPE C.T. and a few H.E 6 Shrapnel shells dropped near the O.B.L. Intelligence. A number of green lights were observed in the direction of F^t COUR d'AVOUE about 3.15 am — red/green lights were also sent up	"Please convey to the officers & men of your command my appreciation of the part they played on there morning of the 28. The cooperation of Your guns was most effective and clear that one team did especially good work in silencing a German machine gun just on the flank of the raiders" Sgd R.I. Macbachlan Brigadier Cdg 112 Bgde
SLOANE SQUARE	28/11/17 to 29/11/17	8.0am to 8.0am	Our offensive. Indirect fire carried out in hostile approaches between 9.30 pm & 3.0 am — Roads being strafed at S29a.6b55 to S23c.50 S23a.01 to S23a.88 S16d.3075 S17c.0055 rounds fired = 7000	

WAR DIARY
or
INTELLIGENCE SUMMARY.
(Erase heading not required.)

Army Form C. 2118.

Place	Date	Hour	Summary of Events and Information	Remarks and references to Appendices
			Hostile Offensive. — Enemy shelled RUE de BOIS and neighbourhood of FACTORY at 3.30 p.m. — One 'plane crossed our line at 11.6 a.m. flying too high for us to fire at it with an anti-aircraft gun mounting.	
SLOANE SQUARE	29/4/17 8.0 am to 30/4/17 8.0 am		The Company was relieved on the morning of the 29th by 63 Company — after handing over the section marched independently to VIELLE CHAPPELLE where the Company went into billets.	
VIELLE CHAPPELLE	30/4/17 8.0 am to 31/4/17		COMPANY in RESERVE BILLETS. General clean up — renewal of clothing — kit inspection — & inspection of spare parts.	
		9.35 am	An unfortunate accident occurred, resulting in the death of No 2. Dance who was accidentally shot owing to the discharge of a revolver which had not been unloaded — full details being forwarded through the usual Channels — a court of enquiry was held — the President being Lt. A.W. Cowle & the members 2/Lt C. Oldhurst 2/Lt. B.H. Brenant all of this company.	

Subject   War Diary

To
H.Q. 112th Inf Bde

Herewith enclosed the War Diary of this Company from 1st of Feb to 28 Feb 1917 Volume XII

please.

Mikefield   [signature] Lt for Major
                                                    O.C.
                        No. 112 M. GUN COMPANY.

Volume XII Feb.

WAR DIARY
or
INTELLIGENCE SUMMARY.
(Erase heading not required.)

Army Form C. 2118.

[Signed] Sam Petching O.C.
No. 142 M. GUN COMPANY.

Vol 12

Place	Date	Hour	Summary of Events and Information	Remarks and references to Appendices
NEILLE CHAPELLE	1.2.19	9 a.m.	Company gun reft fullers parade, inspection, Infantry drill, cleaning limbers and guns. Lecture "map reading"	WJ
		4.30 p.m.		WJ
NEILLE CHAPELLE	2.2.19	9 a.m.	Company in village billets. Parade P.T. Infantry drill Gun drill Routine packs Note Books.	WJ
		4.30 p.m.	Lecture "Esprit de Corps"	WJ
NEILLE CHAPELLE	3.2.19	9.45 a.m.	Company in village billets. Parade P.T. Infantry drill. Gunnery drill. Packhorse limbers & harness & equipment.	WJ
		4.30 p.m.	Lecture "Bells & fuses"	WJ
NEILLE CHAPELLE	4.2.19	9 a.m.	Company in village billets. General inspection by the Major General commanding 4th Div. Inc. Co. & complimented the Company on the condition of the guns.	WJ
		4.30 p.m.	Lecture "Discipline"	WJ
NEILLE CHAPELLE	5.2.19	9 a.m.	Company in reserve billets. Route march. Gun drill	WJ
		4.30 p.m.		WJ
NEILLE CHAPELLE	6.2.19	9 a.m.	Company in reserve billets. Parade P.T. Gun drill. Company drill. Cleaning.	WJ
		4.30 p.m.	Lecture "Discipline"	WJ
NEILLE CHAPELLE	7.2.19	9 a.m.	Company in reserve billets. Parade P.T. Inspection. Company drill.	WJ
		4.30 p.m.		WJ
NEILLE CHAPELLE	8.2.19	9 a.m.	Company in reserve billets. Parade. Packing of stores. Preparation for march.	WJ
		4.30 p.m.		WJ

Army Form C. 2118.

[Signature] O.C.
No. 112 M. GUN COMPANY.

WAR DIARY
or
INTELLIGENCE SUMMARY.
(Erase heading not required.)

Instructions regarding War Diaries and Intelligence Summaries are contained in F.S. Regs., Part II. and the Staff Manual respectively. Title pages will be prepared in manuscript.

Place	Date	Hour	Summary of Events and Information	Remarks and references to Appendices
LES BREBIS.	10.2.19	9 a.m.	Company paraded at 9 am at VIEILLE CHAPELLE and marched to LES BREBIS arriving at 3 p.m. Distance covered 16 miles. The men fell out took ten minutes halt each hour.	WF
LES BREBIS	10.2.19		Two gun teams under LT. R.C. WACE paraded at 9 a.m. and proceeded to their positions in the trenches R.32 and R.33 from 93rd Machine Gun Coy, LT TONKS and 7.1.0 and six men paraded at 4.30 a.m. and proceeded to FOSSE 2 where they took over Anti Aircraft Emplacements from 93rd Machine Gun Coy. At 2 p.m. Company took over billets and Limber from 93rd Company. The two guns at R.32 and R.33 did not fire being in the LOOS defence. The suitable target appeared for the Anti Aircraft gun and all ratified aircraft being out of range. Remainder of the company were employed cleaning up billets.	WF
LES BREBIS	12.2.19	9 a.m.	All men in billets employed on the painting of Limbers and the cleaning of guns. Lecture on Indirect fire by CAPT G. GAUNTLETT to N.C.O.'s. Position R.32 had a direct hit from a 5.9 shell but no damage was caused to the team or gun etc...	WF
LES BREBIS	13.2.19		Relieving to relieve guns R.32 R.33 an at FOSSE 2. Painting of Limbers continued.	WF

T2134. Wt. W708—776. 500000. 4/15. Str J.C. & S.

WAR DIARY or INTELLIGENCE SUMMARY

Army Form C. 2118.

No. 112 M. GUN COMPANY.

Place	Date	Hour	Summary of Events and Information	Remarks and references to Appendices
LES BREBIS	14.2.17		and out and on of day by the section in billets. Was helped indirect fire of all ranks in bullets. Panking of limbers continued. Nothing unusual occurred at R32, R33 and FOSSE 2.	
LES BREBIS	15.2.17	8 am	2 gun teams under 2nd Lt. WOOLFORD and 2nd Lt. BAKER proceeded to the trenches and relieved Lt. WACE and 2 gun teams of No 2 section.	
		12 Noon	22 N.C.Os. and men proceeded to the trenches and were posted in the following positions held by the 9th Cavalry Squadron. This party was under Lt. W. TONKS. 30 N.C.Os. and men proceeded to MAROC. They will form a working party and will complete unfinished emplacements and dug outs. This party under 2nd Lt. T.B. MERRICK. Relieved the 9th L. U. Squadron. R31, R30, S3a, R29, S15, F, S11, S12, R25, R24, R28	
LES BREBIS	16.2.17	10 am	All gun teams and others in the line to billets owing to a Brigade Order which stated this company was to relieve 191 Machine Gun Company in LOOS. Limbers with bombing material packed and sections made ready for the line. Limber and pack animals etc were dispatched at dusk with a guard to LOOS while the limbers but travelled	

WAR DIARY or INTELLIGENCE SUMMARY

Army Form C. 2118.

No. 17 M. GUN COMPANY.

Place	Date	Hour	Summary of Events and Information	Remarks and references to Appendices
LES BREBIS	14.2.14	12 Noon	A guard being mounted on the gun Ausbell &c. Twelve gun teams under Lt. W. TONKS, 2/Lt. MERRICK, 2/Lt. F. McGOWAN left G.H.Q. for LOOS where they relieved twelve guns of 1917 M.G. Relief completed at 8 p.m.	WJ
LES BREBIS	18.2.14		Our guns are purely defensive, and are hidden the control of the Loos commander. No firing is permitted except in the case of an enemy attack. Four gun teams dug out some of the emplacements requiring to be altered enough to had field of fire. Anti-aircraft emplacements were found unsuitable and two new mountings being dug in 100 yds. apart.	WJ
LES BREBIS	19.2.14		This emplacements were lifted and work began on them. Trenches are in a very bad state owing to the thaw and a great amount of draining is required.	WJ
LES BREBIS	20.2.14		Gun at R132 and R133 carried out the following in direct fire. POSITION OF GUN TARGET ROUNDS FIRED. TIME RESULT. R32a M12.B.4.5.4.5 500. 3.10 am Unobserved 3.30 am	WJ

T2134. Wt. W708—776. 500000. 4/15. Sir J. C. & S.

Army Form C. 2118.

WAR DIARY
or
INTELLIGENCE SUMMARY.
(Erase heading not required.)

No. 12 M. GUN COMPANY.

Instructions regarding War Diaries and Intelligence Summaries are contained in F. S. Regs., Part II. and the Staff Manual respectively. Title pages will be prepared in manuscript.

Place	Date	Hour	Summary of Events and Information	Remarks and references to Appendices
			POSITION OF GUN / **TARGET** / **ROUNDS FIRED** / **TIME** / **RESULT**	
			R 32. — M11 c 8.3.1.0 h — 450 — 3.15 am to 3.30 am — Unknown	MAP REF.
			— M1 d 0.0.9.3 — — 3.30 am —	FRANCE
			R 33 — N1 d 2.0.4.0 h — — 3.10 am to 3.20 am — Unknown	SHEET 36c S.W.
			— N1 d 8.0.4.2 — 360 — —	EDITION 2.A.
			R 33. — N4 a 1.0.4.5 h — 450 — 3.15 am to 3.30 am — Unknown	1/20,000
			— N4 c 9.0.1.0 — — —	
			TOTAL ROUNDS 2600	
LES BREBIS	21.2.19		Work was carried out on the new emplacements	West
LES BREBIS	22.2.19		The usual shelling and sniping resumed during the night. Nothing of importance to report.	West
LES BREBIS	23.2.19		Usual trench routine, and work on emplacements. A new nomage scheme was started on with daughter guns in newly constructed emplacements & same time being prepared for same & new guns to relieve the offensive strafing.	West
LES BREBIS	24.2.19		Very quiet. Half the Machine counter battery units and T.M. strafe	West

O.C. Army Form C. 2118.

WAR DIARY
or
INTELLIGENCE SUMMARY.
(Erase heading not required.)

No. 112 M. GUN COMPANY.

Instructions regarding War Diaries and Intelligence Summaries are contained in F. S. Regs., Part II. and the Staff Manual respectively. Title pages will be prepared in manuscript.

Place	Date	Hour	Summary of Events and Information	Remarks and references to Appendices
LES BREBIS	26.2.14	2 p.m.	Work was carried on successfully with the emplacements in front inspection by O.C. Divisional Coy who passed the him and they proved on all respects in order blue.	Out
		11.30 p.m.	WREXHAM TUNNEL. Officer in charge was accidentally blown up at Tunnel P.O.P on a short time [?] entered with was started at face with spot about ran to dig them out with the help of the 9th NORTH STAFFORDS (PIONEERS) thoroughly assisted in digging and a strong hopes were held out of eventually rescuing the men.	
LES BREBIS	27.2.14		Experienced a moment but were replaced by some with the assistance of the R.E.S. but great difficulty it experienced in shoring up the dug nothing [?] has to the depth	Out
LES BREBIS	24.2.14		The above party have had been dug out and a little later of putting the men a fresh area to avail was after an hour left the surface	Out
LES BREBIS	28.2.14	11.30 a.m.	the body of Sgt Ingham was left in Ga B. Coy	Out
LES BREBIS	28.2.14	12 p.m.	Gun teams on Anti Aircraft duties relieved by 11th Motor Machine	

Army Form C. 2118.

WAR DIARY
or
INTELLIGENCE SUMMARY.
(Erase heading not required.)

Instructions regarding War Diaries and Intelligence Summaries are contained in F. S. Regs., Part II. and the Staff Manual respectively. Title pages will be prepared in manuscript.

No. 103 M. GUN COMPANY

Place	Date	Hour	Summary of Events and Information	Remarks and references to Appendices
		5 p.m.	The Battalion Relief completed at 2.30 p.m. This 1 of 12 Gun teams from 103 Machine Gun Coy proceeded to the Trenches to hour the line in areas of the Relief on the approach to the Village of the willing-men, but work still going on at full pressure.	

YM/3

SECRET

WAR DIARY
of
110th MACHINE GUN COMPANY

1st of March to 31st of March 1917

(VOLUME XIII)

… O.C.
No. 112 M... N COMPANY.

WAR DIARY
or
INTELLIGENCE SUMMARY.
(Erase heading not required.)

Army Form C. 2118.

Place	Date	Hour	Summary of Events and Information	Remarks and references to Appendices
LES BREBIS	1/3/1914	1 p.m.	Guides reported at C.H.Q. from each gun team in the line and attacked themselves to 192 Machine Gun Coy. who then proceeded to the trenches. Relief completed without a hitch our guns being ready to move off at 5 p.m. All gun teams arrived in billets before 9 p.m.	Auf
		10 p.m.	WREXHAM TUNNEL being carried on by 192 Machine Gun Coy.	Auf
LES BREBIS	2/3/14	9 a.m.	General clean up of Company Guns, transport, spare parts, ammunition & being overhauled. Clothing finished to renew what kilmits re-	
		4.30 p.m.	bundled and landed.	
LES BREBIS	3/3/14	9 a.m.	Company paraded outside billets and marched off to an area around VERQUINEUL. Distance approx. 5½ miles. To men	Auf
		12 noon	fell out. 192 Machine Gun Company reported the finding of the men attached in WREXHAM TUNNEL. Put at hang dead and the others kin alive to the Dressing Station.	
VERQUINEUL	4/3/14	8.30 a.m.	Company moved off and paraded to ROBECQ.	Auf
		1 p.m.	Arrived in billets all Distance approx. 10 miles. To men fell out.	Auf
ROBECQ	5/3/14	8.30 a.m.	Company paraded and marched to Nē DONCHELLE.	Auf
		2 p.m.	Arrived in billets. Distance covered 13½ miles. The men fell out.	Auf

Army Form C. 2118.

WAR DIARY
or
INTELLIGENCE SUMMARY.
(Erase heading not required.)

No. 12 M. GUN COMPANY.

Instructions regarding War Diaries and Intelligence Summaries are contained in F. S. Regs., Part II. and the Staff Manual respectively. Title pages will be prepared in manuscript.

Place	Date	Hour	Summary of Events and Information	Remarks and references to Appendices
NEDONCHELLE	6/5/19	10.0 a.m	Company at rest. Cleaning guns repacking limbers. P.T. and Recreation.	aus
		4:30 pm	Inspection.	aus
NEDONCHELLE	14/5/19	9.0 am	Company drill. P.T. Lumber drill. Football match.	aus
		4:30 pm		aus
NEDONCHELLE	8/5/19	9.30 am	Company moved off to new billeting area in accordance with programme. Owned in billets. Distance covered 11 miles. No men fell out	aus
ANTIN	9/5/19	9.30 am	Company paraded and marched to training area. Weather conditions about it all. Guns and limber.	aus
		3.30 pm	Owned in billets. Distance covered 16½ miles. No men fell out.	aus
REBREUVIETTE	10/5/19	10-0 am	Company and section gun cleaning	aus
		12.30 pm		
REBREUVIETTE	11/5/19	10.30 am	Church parade.	aus
REBREUVIETTE	12/5/19	9.0 am	Intensive training commenced. Squad drill. Company drill. Gas drill. (advanced) gun cleaning. Football. Boxing. Lecture. The use of the Lombard. Lt C. PALMER	aus
		6 pm		
REBREUVIETTE	13/5/19	9.0 am	Company drill. gun drill. T.A. mechanism. Bomb throwing. P.T. Football	aus
		6.0 pm	Lecture "Open fighting as applied to machine guns" 2nd Lt F. McGOWAN.	aus

WAR DIARY
or
INTELLIGENCE SUMMARY.

(Erase heading not required.)

Army Form C. 2118.

_____ O.C.
No. 112 M. GUN COMPANY.

Place	Date	Hour	Summary of Events and Information	Remarks and references to Appendices
REBREUVIETTE	14/3/19	9.0 am	Company drill. Arm drill. P.T. Sports. Lecture "The value of Indirect Fire"	
		6.0 pm	2/Lt. T. B. MERRICK.	
		11.30 pm	Night Operations. Rampart leaving 9.5	
		11.30 pm		
REBREUVIETTE	15/3/14	9.0 am	Schemes. "Pack saddle" 2/Lt. B. H. DURRANT.	
		11.50 pm	Lecture.	
REBREUVIETTE	16/3/14	9.0 am	Range practice. Gun tests. Rifle practice.	
		11.40 pm	Lecture "Overhead fire" 2nd Lt. J. PENMAN.	
		5.0 pm		
REBREUVIETTE	17/3/14	9.0 am	Brigade route march.	
		6.0 pm	Night operations.	
		8.0 pm	Church parade.	
REBREUVIETTE	18/3/14	9.0 am	Company paraded and marched off to new billeting area.	
		2.0 pm	Arrived in billets. Distance covered 4½ miles.	
		5.30 pm	Instruction on compass work.	
HOUVIGNEUL	19/3/14	9.0 am	Parading of guns.	
		2.0 pm		
		5.0 pm	Lecture "The M.G.O. in Indirect fire" Lt. R.C. WACE.	

WAR DIARY
or
INTELLIGENCE SUMMARY.
(Erase heading not required.)

Army Form C. 2118.

[signature] O.C.
112 M. GUN COMPANY.

Place	Date	Hour	Summary of Events and Information	Remarks and references to Appendices
HOUVIGNEUL	20/3/19	9.0.a.m	Instruction on Elevation, directing dial, elevating dial, spirit level	[sig]
		12.0 p.m	Pack saddle work.	[sig]
		5.0 p.m	Lecture "Rheumatism" Lt. A.W. CARLE.	
HOUVIGNEUL	21/3/19	8.30 a.m	Company route march. Distance covered 13 miles.	[sig]
		6 p.m	Lecture, to N.C.O.s, "Discipline" 2nd Lt. C. PALMER.	
HOUVIGNEUL	22/3/19	9.0.a.m	Barrage fire.	[sig]
		12.N.		
		2.0 p.m	Lecture "Aircraft" 2nd Lt. F. McGOWAN.	
		4 p.m		
		7.0 p.m	Night operations.	
		10.0 p.m		
NOUVIGNEUL	23/3/19	9.0 a.m	Company drill. Gun drill.	[sig]
		1.0 p.m		
		2.0 p.m	Mechanism. Cleaning guns.	
		4.0 p.m		
HOUVIGNEUL	24/3/19	7.30 a.m	Brigade route march. Distance covered 14 miles.	[sig]
		7.0 p.m	Night operations.	
		9.0 p.m		

WAR DIARY
or
INTELLIGENCE SUMMARY.

Army Form C. 2118.

No. 112 M. Gun Company

Place	Date	Hour	Summary of Events and Information	Remarks and references to Appendices
HOUVIGNEUL	25/3/14	9.0.a.m	Church parade.	
HOUVIGNEUL	26/3/14	9.0.a.m	Bosnage fire. Hands etc on pack animals.	
		12.30 pm	Open fighting and Lewis gun drill.	
		2.0 pm		
		4 pm	Open fighting and Lewis gun drill.	
HOUVIGNEUL	27/3/14	9.0.am	Bosnage fire. Pack saddle drill.	
		1.30 pm	Company route march. Distance covered 10 miles.	
		2 pm		
		4.0 pm		
HOUVIGNEUL	28/3/14	9.0.am	Company mechanism. I.A. Lewis gun drill. Belt filling.	
HOUVIGNEUL	29/3/14	9.am	Bosnage fire. Pack animals.	
		12.30 pm		
		2.0 pm		
		4.0 pm		
HOUVIGNEUL	30/3/14	10.0.am	Company left Houville to take part in a practice Brigade attack. Pack animals were used and formed a useful suggestion in carrying all that was required for an attack with the help of 86 attached men.	
		4.30 pm	Company returned to billets.	

Army Form C. 2118.

[signature] O.C.
No. 112 M. GUN COMPANY.

WAR DIARY
or
INTELLIGENCE SUMMARY.
(Erase heading not required.)

Instructions regarding War Diaries and Intelligence Summaries are contained in F. S. Regs., Part II. and the Staff Manual respectively. Title pages will be prepared in manuscript.

Place	Date	Hour	Summary of Events and Information	Remarks and references to Appendices
HOUVIGNEUL	31/3/18	9.0 am to 12.0 pm	Company drill.	
		12.0 to 1.0	Cleaning guns.	

XIV

CONFIDENTIAL

Vol/14

WAR DIARY
of
113th MACHINE GUN COMPANY
1st of APRIL TO 30th of APRIL 1917

(VOLUME XIV)

Subject   War Diary

To/ H.Q.
112th M.G.B.C.

Herewith Pleasefind
War Diary for the month of
April 1917. of 112th Machine
Gun Company.

       Volume ~~XIVI~~

                      phase

In the field   W. Fouks. Lt & Adjt
1/5/17   112th M.G. Coy.

Army Form C. 2118.

WAR DIARY
or
INTELLIGENCE SUMMARY.
(Erase heading not required.)

Instructions regarding War Diaries and Intelligence Summaries are contained in F. S. Regs., Part II. and the Staff Manual respectively. Title pages will be prepared in manuscript.

Place	Date	Hour	Summary of Events and Information	Remarks and references to Appendices
HOUVIGNEUL	1/4/14	9.0.a.m	Church Parade. LT.R.C.WACE LT. W. TONKS, LT. F. McGOWAN, LT. C. PALMER & LT. R.C.WACE Brigade Headquarters to reconnoitre the line in front of ARRAS.	aus
		4.0 p.m	The above whole returning from the line and when passing through the STATION a shell burst wounding LT. F. McGOWAN in the right foot. LT. TONKS and LT. WACE assisted by LT. PALMER carried him to the nearest dressing station.	aus
HOUVIGNEUL	2/4/14	9.0.a.m	Open fighting pack animals being used.	aus
		12.30 p.m	"	
		2.0 p.m	Mechanism Belt filling & leaving gun &	
		4.30 p.m	"	
		5.0 p.m	Lecture. "First aid" LT. R.C. WACE.	
HOUVIGNEUL	3/4/14	9.0.a.m	Range. Parti Table C. being fired.	aus
		4.30 p.m	"	
HOUVIGNEUL	8/4/14	9.0.a.m	Preparing for the line. Inspection by Section officers.	aus
		12.30 p.m	"	
		2.0 p.m	Packing limbers	
		4.0 p.m	"	
HOUVIGNEUL	5/4/14	4.30 a.m	Company moved off to new billeting area.	aus
		1.0 p.m	Arrived in Killette. Distance covered 16 miles	

WAR DIARY
or
INTELLIGENCE SUMMARY.
(Erase heading not required.)

Army Form C. 2118.

Place	Date	Hour	Summary of Events and Information	Remarks and references to Appendices
HABARCQ.	6/4/14	9.0.a.m to 12.30 p.m	Alteration of duties. Eighty attached men instructed in hill filling	
		2.0 pm to 5.0 pm	Lecture by section officers, giving a insight into the operations.	
			Two Guns would play their the operations.	
HABARCQ.	7/4/14	9.0.a.m to 12.30 pm	Company drill. Gun drill. Cleaning guns.	
		2.0 pm	Football match.	
		3.0 pm	LT. A.W. CARLE with 2/LT. S. PALMER left for ARRAS to reconnoitre LONDON CAVE. Operation Orders issued by MAJOR H. G. GAUNTLETT. Commanding 112th Machine Gun Coy.	

REFERENCE MAPS. Scale 1/20,000. 51 B. S.W. and 51 B. N.W. Also special maps.

ATTACK ON MONCHY-LE-PREUX.

Object of the attack of the 112th Infantry Brigade are:—
a) To sieze the spurs South of MONCHY-LE-PREUX, running to the west of the line 0.1.C.23 to N.12.C.9.5.40.
b) To make good the line from N12.C.9.2. to O4.B.4.5. 9.5.
c) To occupy the village of GUEMAPPE.

TIME OF ATTACK. Attack will take place after the leading Divisions have

WAR DIARY
or
INTELLIGENCE SUMMARY.

(Erase heading not required.)

Army Form C. 2118.

Place	Date	Hour	Summary of Events and Information	Remarks and references to Appendices
			taken the BROWN LINE and are established on the high ground about ORANGE and CHAPEL hills. The attack will depend upon the time the artillery can get forward. Probably ZERO + 10 hours.	
			FORMING 3/ The Brigade will be formed up on the line running north UP. and South through HEUCHY CHAPELLE from H 33 d.9.8 to N 5 d 4.6. in a front of 1,200 yards.	
			FRONT LINE. The 6th BEDFORDSHIRE REGT., RIGHT. " 8th EAST LANCS., REGT. LEFT. " 10th LOYAL NORTH LANCS. REGT. IN SUPPORT " 11th ROYAL WARWICKS., REGT. IN RESERVE. Dividing point between Battalions N 5 b 4.5.	
			OBJECTIVES:- The 6th Bedfordshire Regt., objective N 12 c 9.0 2.5 to WINDMILL N 12 b 4.1.(inclusive) When this line is secured they will occupy GUEMAPPE village and connect with VII Corps. The 8th East Lancs. Regt. Objective N 4 b 2.1. exclusive to O 4 b H.5. 9.5. connecting with 10th ROYAL FUSILIERS on their left.	

WAR DIARY
or
INTELLIGENCE SUMMARY.

(Erase heading not required.)

Army Form C. 2118.

10th LOYAL NORTH LANCS REGT., can reinforce when of these Battalions
11th ROYAL WARWICK, REGT., Echelon in rear of 10th LOYAL NORTH LANCS
and keep in touch with the leading Battalion protecting
our right flank.

No 3 On advancing from the assembly position No 3 Section
SECTION. under LT. W. TONKS will follow directly behind 8th EAST LANCS REGT.

No 2 Section under 2/LT. J. S. PENMAN will follow the 6th BEDFORDS
SECTION. On reaching the BROWN LINE these two sections will establish
themselves at CHAPEL HILL and open BARRAGE fire on the advance
of an infantry. Detail orders for the barrage fire are
issued in appendix.

No 1 No 1 Section under 2/LT. C.R.B. WOOLFORD will remain in Brigade
SECTION. reserve and move in rear of the left flank of the 11th
ROYAL WARWICKS, REGT.,

No. 4 No 4 Section under LT. R.C. WACE and 2/LT. W.V. BAKER will
SECTION. move in rear of the right flank of the 11th ROYAL WARWICKS.

WAR DIARY
or
INTELLIGENCE SUMMARY.
(Erase heading not required.)

Army Form C. 2118.

On reaching the BROWN LINE they will advance in rear of the 8th EAST LANCS. REGT. and establish themselves on the outskirts of MONCHY-LE-PREUX about O.1.C.4. protecting the front of the 8th EAST LANCS.

PERSONNEL and EQUIPMENT. Each gun team should be ten in number, with one extra number being carried from the tank in charge of the Brigade Infantry. The two drivers will accompany each limbered G.S. wagon. Each team will take the following limits gun team, 1 Pair lamps, 1 spare parts, 14 boxes of ammunition (full boxes), 1 Petrol tin full of water, condensor and tube, oil can, spare ammunition, carrier gun carrier. Barrage guns will take one belt filling machine and one Vickers finder per section.

The 1st section will dump right half, hopper bar gun, at FEUCHY CHAPELLE. Nos 2 and 3 sections will dump there. The reserve section will leave the man at the dump

WAR DIARY
or
INTELLIGENCE SUMMARY.

(Erase heading not required.)

Army Form C. 2118.

until all these hill have have been withdrawn by the evening of June.

Coy H.Q. Advance parties will follow in rear of the two leading Battalions and establish themselves in the vicinity of CHAPEL HILL, a black and white chequered flag will mark the exact spot.

COMMUNICATIONS: Communication between Section Officers and Coy. H.Q. will be by runner. All runners will carry filled message forms in top left pocket.

RATIONS: The Company will carry two days rations with them, and the unexpended portion of 2 days ration Return parties will meet and draw rations on the night of Z+1 day from the dump at FEUCHY CHAPELLE. Rations will be at that dump every night.

AMMUNITION: Ammunition will be drawn from Brigade dump at FEUCHY CHAPELLE.

WAR DIARY
or
INTELLIGENCE SUMMARY.

Army Form C. 2118.

WATER. Patrol 8ans will be sent up with rations. Ration parties must always hand in an empty tin when drawing a full tin of water.

TIME TABLE.

Z-1 hour. Company marching towards EQUIPMENT DUMP.

Z+1 hour. Arrive at EQUIPMENT DUMP. One day's rations issued. Off load arms etc. from limbers on to pack animals. Hot meal will be taken. Lt. A.W. CARLE to report to Brigade Head quarters.
MAP REF., G 26 b a.a. Appox.,

Z+3 hour. Company will proceed in rear of ROYAL WARWICKS REGT, to assembly area.

Z+5 hours Arrive in LONDON CAVE. Pack mules will be taken under cover in houses in the vicinity.

Z+6 hours Company will get into position ready for the advance.
40 minutes.

WAR DIARY or INTELLIGENCE SUMMARY

Army Form C. 2118.

Place	Date	Hour	Summary of Events and Information	Remarks and references to Appendices
HABARCQ.	9/4/19	9.0 a.m.	Company paraded and moved off towards the line.	Gauntlett
		11.0 a.m.	Arrived at WARLUS.	
		1.0 p.m.	Lecture to N.C.Os dealing with the attack by MAJOR H.G. GAUNTLETT.	
		9.0 p.m.	Synchronized watches. Received final orders from Brigade and ZERO hour.	
WARLUS	9/4/19	4.0 a.m.	Left WARLUS and proceeded to EQUIPMENT DUMP.	
		5:30 a.m.	Our Artillery started a heavy bombardment on the Enemy.	
		6:30 a.m.	Arrived at EQUIPMENT DUMP. Drew rations tea & a hot meal. Weather very bad. Rain and sleet. Unloaded lorries, dumped trusses etc. etc. Lorries loaded on to pack mules.	
		10:30 a.m.	Brigade moved off towards ARRAS.	
		11.00 a.m.	ARRAS STATION heavily shelled. One direct hit exploding an ammunition dump; one man in the Company being wounded.	
		11:30 a.m.	Arrived at LONDON CAVE. Mules being placed under cover in a gun horse.	
		2:15 p.m.	Company left the assembly area and moved up into position astride the CAMBRAI ROAD, in our original front line.	
		5.0 p.m.	The Company moved into barrage towards the BROWN LINE.	
		5:45 p.m.	On coming over the ridge west of BOIS DES BOEUFS the enemy shelled the	

WAR DIARY
or
INTELLIGENCE SUMMARY.
(Erase heading not required.)

Army Form C. 2118.

Place	Date	Hour	Summary of Events and Information	Remarks and references to Appendices
		6:15 p.m.	Company with 3.9 howitzers. A temporary halt was made in the BOIS DES BOEUFS. The guns and ammunition etc., were unloaded and the mules returned to the transport lines West of ARRAS.	
		6:20 p.m.	The BOIS DES BOEUFS was heavily shelled ca. 70 r further during 11. O.R. wounded.	
		11.0 p.m	The attack on the BROWN LINE was postponed. The Company were ordered up in artillery formation astride the CAMBRAI ROAD, to within 800 yds of the BROWN LINE where emplacements were made and the guns dug in mounted. The 14 inch action remaining in reserve at the BOIS DES BOEUFS.	
	10/4/17.	3.50 a.m.	Orders were received from Brigade Headquarters that no further advance would be made on FEUCHY CHAPEL position till 8.15 am and that the Brigade would withdraw to the West of MAISON ROUGE. The Company remained in this position.	
		12.0 NOON.	The attack was postponed until 12 NOON. The attack on FEUCHY CHAPEL and the BROWN LINE commenced. The 12th Division attacked supported by the 34th Division.	
		2.0 p.m	No 3. Section under LT. W. TONKS and No. 2 Section under 2"PLT. J.S. PENMAN	

WAR DIARY or INTELLIGENCE SUMMARY

Army Form C. 2118.

Place	Date	Hour	Summary of Events and Information	Remarks and references to Appendices
			moved up swiftly passed through our infantry and reached the Eastern slope of CHAPEL HILL with the first wave of the attacking infantry of the 12th Division, and placed their guns in position and advanced. Nos 2 section, No 2 light was of No. 3. The guns were ready to open barrage fire on the advance of the 34th Division to the time guns had already received orders to put up a barrage from ORANGE and CHAPEL HILLS on the 34th Divisional objective including GUE'MAPPE. As only guns of No. 2 and No. 3 sections came into position. MONCHY LE PREUX and GUE'MAPPE were barraged under this barrage the 34th Division advanced. The guns of these section kept up a steady fire during the attack until 4.0 p.m. firing 30,000 rounds. No 4 section under Lt. R. C. WACE and 2nd Lt. W. V. BAKER advanced with the 8th EAST LANCS. REGT, the left leading battalion, No 1 section under 2nd Lt. C.R.B. WOOLFORD moved up in rear & west of FEUCHY CHAPEL.	
		5.0 pm	Infantry requested the Company to return. Their barrage as they were right of the enemy advancing. Fire was opened and kept up for 1 hour	

WAR DIARY or INTELLIGENCE SUMMARY

Army Form C. 2118.

Place	Date	Hour	Summary of Events and Information	Remarks and references to Appendices
		5.30 p.m.	No 4 Section opened fire on enemy patrol and the open running South from MONCHY. The advance was resumed.	
		6.0 p.m.		
		8.26 p.m.	LIEUT. R.C. WACE was wounded and 2nd LT. W.V. BAKER took command of the Section.	
		8.30 p.m.	Received word the enemy were counter attacking from GUÉMAPPE. Nos 2 and 3 Sect. and opened fire, and Rifle Wpt of barrage for ½ hour at LES FOSSES FARM.	W.J.
	9.0 p.m.	The 112th Bde retired to its old position as its flanks were open.	
10/4/17		5.0 a.m.	The advance was resumed. No 2 Sect under 2/Lt J.S. PENMAN advanced to support the right Battn (16th BEDFORDS REGT) and No 4 Sect continued to advance with the Left Batt (10 & 2 IN.J) Nos 1 + 3 Sects. advanced in support to the Brigade.	
		5.30 a.m. 5.45 a.m.	2/Lt J.S. PENMAN was wounded. The object was gained, as shown in map D, during this advance all sections suffered heavily from shell fire and enemy machine gun fire from GUÉMAPPE. No 4 Sect lost one gun and team blown to pieces.	
		8.30 a.m.	Nos 3 + 1 Sects. opened fire on an enemy collecting for counter attack at O.7c in Sunken Rd South of CAMBRAI ROAD - firing for ½ hour.	
		2.15 p.m.	No 4 Sect fired on GUÉMAPPE 20 minutes to support attack of 3rd Div. Enemy mounted troops east of GUÉMAPPE were scattered.	
		2.55 p.m.	The 112 Bde were counter attacked by the enemy infantry from GUÉMAPPE. 110 Sect	

WAR DIARY or INTELLIGENCE SUMMARY.

Army Form C. 2118.

(Erase heading not required.)

Instructions regarding War Diaries and Intelligence Summaries are contained in F. S. Regs., Part II. and the Staff Manual respectively. Title pages will be prepared in manuscript.

Signed: Launcelot War(?)

Place	Date	Hour	Summary of Events and Information	Remarks and references to Appendices
		4.45pm	opened fire with their two right guns. The counterattack broke down 400 ft from our line and the enemy halted. Lt. M.V. BAKER was wounded in the arm, but remained at duty.	
		5.0pm	The enemy counter attacked again and attempted to dig-in. Our artillery opened fire, and the enemy bolted again. During the counterattack one gun and team of No 4 Sec. were blown to pieces.	
		6.0pm	2/Lt M.V. BAKER in touch with 111Bde.	
		7.0pm	The enemy counterattacked weakly. They never developed. Orders of relief were received. Coy was relieved by 36 MGC	WJ
ARRAS	12/4/17	6.0pm	The Company was collected in billets in ARRAS	
		11am	The company returned to billets in ARRAS. During the operations some 50,000 rounds were fired	
WANQUETIN	14/4/17	9.0pm	Moved by Motor Bus to WANQUETIN, in Billets for two nights	WJ
	15/4/17	11.30am	Moved to DENIER in rest billets	WJ
DENIER	18/4/17		In rest billets at DENIER. Time spent in cleaning up & refitting	WJ
	19/4/17	10.0am	Marched to Billets in NOVELLETTE and stayed two days – cleaning up and preparing for the line	WJ
NOVELLETTE	21/4/17	10.30am	Moved into bivouacs in the old English front line at G.11.d.8.6 (51 S.W.) & stayed the night	WJ
	22/4/17	4.20 Am & 8.0pm	Morning – Time spent in cleaning up & seeing essentials for the line section moved off at intervals for the POINT de JOUR, where they were in support dept at G.11.d.8.6.	WJ

WAR DIARY or INTELLIGENCE SUMMARY

Army Form C. 2118.

Place	Date	Hour	Summary of Events and Information	Remarks and references to Appendices
LE POINT DE JOUR	23/4/17	4.45am	No 1 & 3 Sections commenced barrage fire from H17.d.8.6. according to programme. The barrage was kept up for 46 minutes. Some 30,000 rounds were fired.	
		7.30am	The 112th Inf Bde commenced to advance from trenches in the vicinity of LE POINT DE JOUR.	
		9.00am	Nos 2 & 4 Sections advanced with the leading Battalion. 63rd Bgde were held up upon the right in CHILI TRENCH. The 6th BEDFORDS and No 4 Section went up in support.	
		10.15am	No 4 Section took up a position round the line I.70.a.28 and opened fire on large bunches of enemy on GREENLAND HILL, firing about 2000 rounds when they advanced.	
		10.30am	Nos 1 & 3 Sections opened barrage fire on enemy collecting in D.B. The enemy retired in a S.E. direction, then reformed and again advanced. Fire was reopened and they again retired, some 2000 rounds were fired.	
		5.45pm	The three remaining Battalions formed up with No 2 Section in HURRAH TRENCH H.6.c preparatory to an attack on GREENLAND HILL.	
		6.00pm	The 112 Bde less one Battalion had reached the ROEUX—GAVRELLE ROAD and were occupying it. No 2 Section was in position at H.12.a and b protecting the front.	
		7.0pm	No 2 Section moved up to CLYDE TRENCH.	
		9.0pm	Nos 1 & 3 Sections advanced to a position about H.12.a & H.12.b reached by No 2 Section.	
		11.0pm	No 1 Sect. + 2 guns of No 3 Section gun into position for the attack next morning (which was cancelled).	W.F.

WAR DIARY or INTELLIGENCE SUMMARY

Army Form C. 2118.

(Signature) Lawrence(?)

Place	Date	Hour	Summary of Events and Information	Remarks and references to Appendices
	24.4.17		No 1 Sect & 2 guns of No 3 Section at H12c5.9. Throughout this day fired on parties of the enemy in GREEN LAND HILL (when they collected in groups of more than five). The troops were principally during the morning	W/3
		9.0 pm	16th L.N. LANCS. REGT. relieved the 63rd Bde. No 2 Section moved up with them and took up their position at about point 6.5. on the ROEUX - GAVRELLE ROAD	
	25.4.17	3.00 am	Both the enemy's and our S.O.S. signals went up on an hight in the direction of ROEUX. No 1 Sect & 2 guns of No 3 opened fire on south side of GREENLAND HILL and kept on till about 4.30 am, firing some 17,000 rounds	
	26.4.17		During the day no parties of the enemy appeared. No 1 Sect fired at enemy aeroplanes whenever they appeared. On one occasion a plane appeared to be hit. During the night No 1 Sect relieved No 1 Section and No 3 Section relieved No 2	W/3
	27.4.17		Enemy aeroplane again fired on during this day. During the night the Coy got into position ready for the attack at Oppy	W/3
		4.25 am	Barrage fire opened & the Bde. began to advance	

Army Form C. 2118.

WAR DIARY
or
INTELLIGENCE SUMMARY.
(Erase heading not required.)

Instructions regarding War Diaries and Intelligence Summaries are contained in F.S. Regs., Part II. and the Staff Manual respectively. Title pages will be prepared in manuscript.

Place	Date	Hour	Summary of Events and Information	Remarks and references to Appendices
[in the field]	28/4/17	Dawn	During the day No.3 Section moved 2 guns to communication trench between CLASP & CUBA trenches firing on the Railway embankment and on enemy M Guns on ridge four throughout the day	
		Midnight	From midnight onwards the Bee was relieved night of the Machine Gun Coy	
	29/4/17		The Coy was relieved during the night 29/30 April & arrived in Bivouac between 2-10 pm 30th April	(5)
ARRAS	30.4.17	5.50 pm	Moved by motor busses to billets in DENIER	(5)

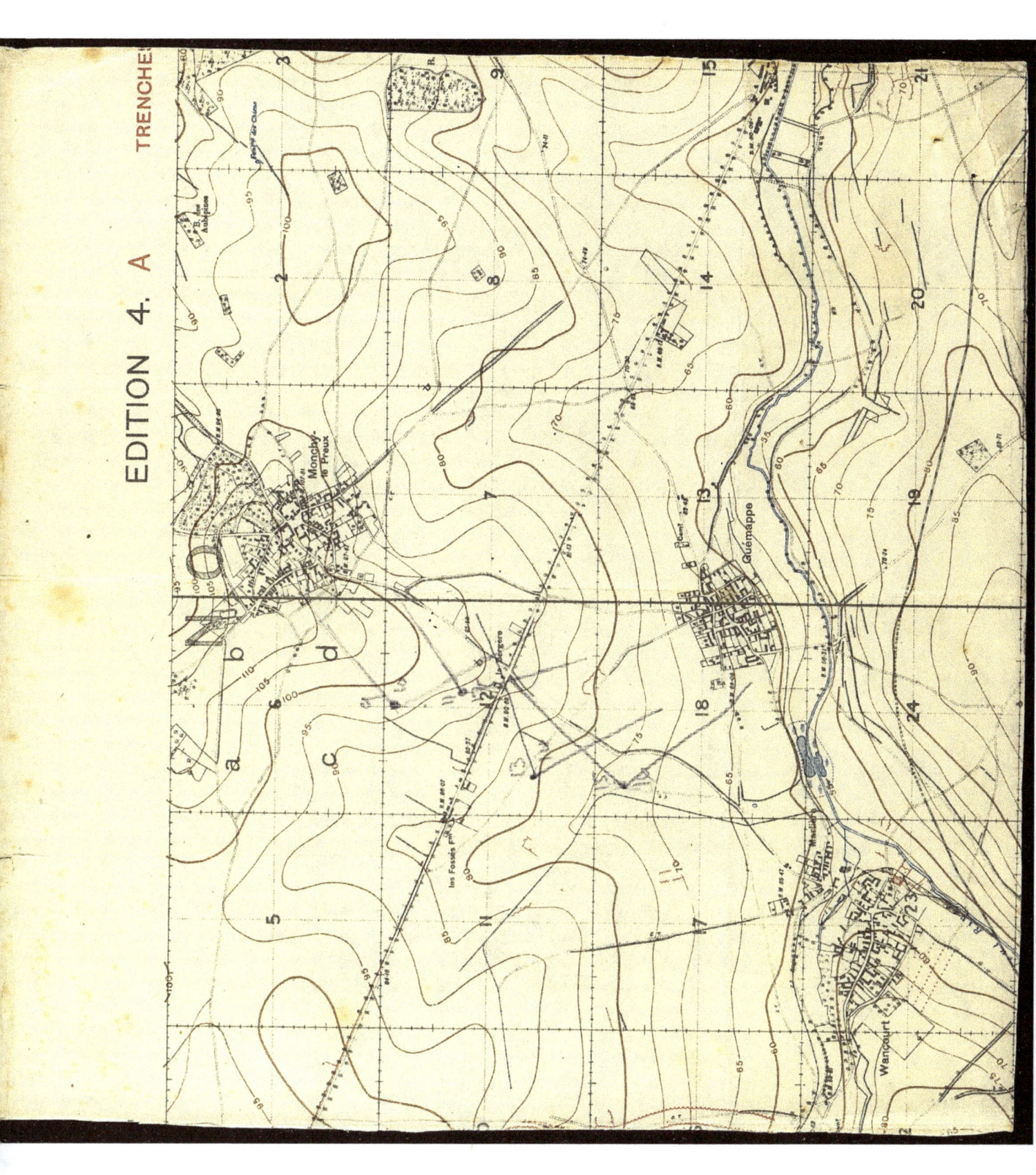

Coron	Workmen's dwellings.
Cour des marchandises, aux	Goods yard.
Couvent	Convent.
Crassier	Slag heap.
Croix	Cross.
Darse	Inner dock.
Démoli - e	Destroyed.
Détruit - e, Dét - v	"
Déversoir	Weir.
Digue	Dyke, causeway.
Distillerie, Dis^te	Distillery.
Douane	Custom-house.
Bureau de douane	"
Entrepôt de douane	Custom warehouse.
Dynamitière, Dynam^re	Dynamite magazine.
Dynamiterie	Dynamite factory.
Écluse	Sluice, Lock.
Éclusette, Écl^te	Sluice.
École	School.
Écurie	Stable.
Église	Church.
Émaillerie	Enamel works.
Embarcadère, Emb^re	Landing-place.
Estaminet, Estam^t	Inn.
Étang	Pond.
Fabrique, Fab^e	Factory.
Fab^e de produits chimiques	Chemical works.
Fab^e de faïence	Pottery.
Faïencerie	"
Ferme, F^me	Farm.
Filature, F^l^re	Spinning mill.
Fonderie, Fond^ie	Foundry.
Fontaine, Font^ne	Spring, fountain.
Forêt	Forest.
Forme de radoub	Dry dock.
Forge	Smithy.
Fosse	Mine, Pit.
Fossé	Moat, Ditch.
Four	Kiln.
" à chaux	Lime-kiln.
Four à coke	Coke oven.
Ganterie	Glove Factory
Gare	Station.
Garenne	Warren.
Garnison	Garrison.
Gazomètre	Gasometer.
Glacerie	Mirror Factory.
Fab^e de glaces	"
Glacière	Ice factory.
Grue	Crane.
Gué	Ford.
Guérite	Sentry-box, Turret.
" à signaux	Signal-box (Ry.)
Halte	Halt.
Hangar	Shed, Hangar.
Hôpital	Hospital.
Hôtel-de-Ville	Town hall.
Houillère	Colliery.
Huilerie	Oil factory.
Imprimerie, Imp^rie	Printing works.
Jetée	Pier.
Laminerie	Rolling mills.
Ligne de haute marée	High water mark.
Laisse de basse marée	Low " "
Maison Forestière, Mon. F^re	Forester's house.
Malterie	Malt-house.
Marbrerie	Marble works.
Marais	Marsh.
Marais salant	Salt marsh.
Marché	Market.
Mare	Pool.
Meule	Rick.
Minière	Mine.
Monastère	Monastery.
Moulin, M^in	Mill.
" à vapeur	Steam mill.
Mur	Wall.
" crénelé	Loop-holed wall.

SECRET

WAR DIARY Vol 15

of

112th MACHINE GUN COMPANY

1st MAY 1917 TO 31st MAY 1917

(VOLUME XV)

WAR DIARY or **INTELLIGENCE SUMMARY**

Army Form C. 2118.

(Erase heading not required.)

W. Tonks Lieut

Place	Date	Hour	Summary of Events and Information	Remarks and references to Appendices
DENIER	1/5/17		Company in rest billets. Following reinforcement received from the Base, 2nd Lt S.C.C. Huggill	C.O.
	2/5/17		4/5 other ranks duly taken on strength to replace casualties. 2nd Lieut W.V. BAKER admitted to hospital suffering from wound received in action 11/4/17.	C.O.
	4/5/17		Lieut A.W. CARLE (2nd in command) evacuated sick & struck off the strength, authority 3rd Army List No 70, dated 4/5/17.	C.O.
	7/5/17		2nd Lieut A.V. HADEN arrived to replace casualty & was taken on the strength	C.O.
	8/5/17		15 other ranks arrived to replace casualties bringing the total effective strength of the Company to:- 11 officers 202 other ranks. Transport of Divisional Lewis Gun Competition held at LIGNEREUIL. M.G. Competition result	C.O.
	9/5/17		112 M.G.C. (1) 687 marks. 111 M.G.C. 622 marks. 63 M.G.C. 617 marks.	C.O.
	13/5/17		Brigade Church Parade at AMBRINES	C.O.
MONTENESCOURT	18/5/17		Company received orders to move from DENIER to MONTENESCOURT and arrived at the last named place the same day.	C.O.
TILLOY	19/5/17		Major Bancroft left for a course at CAMIERS, Lieut W. TONKS taking over command of the Company. 2nd Lieut C. PALMER acting 2nd in command. Lieut W. TONKS, 2nd Lieut C. PALMER & Lieut C.R. WOOLFORD proceeded to TILLOY the first two going on to the Coy H.Q. of 167 Company & 143 M.G.C. at N.11.a.2.6 Map 51B S.W. 2 Scale 1:10,000. Lieut WOOLFORD remaining at TILLOY to arrange accommodation for the Company. Lieut TONKS & 2nd Lieut Palmer reconnoitred the Wagon Lines and Gun positions and arranged for W.P. the Company arrived at TILLOY and took over bivouacs between DEVILS WOOD & TILLOY (north of ARRAS-WANCOURT ROAD.)	C.O.

WAR DIARY
or
INTELLIGENCE SUMMARY.

Army Form C. 2118.

M. Winkop/end

Place	Date	Hour	Summary of Events and Information	Remarks and references to Appendices
TILLOY	20/5/17	2.00am	No 3 & 4 Section moved into support of 167 M.G. Coy.	C.O.
		9.0pm	2 teams of No 4 Section relieved 2 teams of 167 M.G.Coy taking one position at N.12.B.65	
	21/5/17		B. afternoon of the 21st under the Co.'s M.G.O. the machine gun defence system was altered and the Company, after completion of relief took up the following position:- O.7.B.2.2 (2guns) B.7.B.75.25 (1gun) O.7.D.5.2 (2guns) O.13.B.25 (2guns) D.19.A.75 (2guns). Here 9 guns formed a belt of fire for the front line defences. The rear line defence guns were placed at N.12.B.08 (2guns) N.12.B.13 (2guns) N.12.C.26 (2guns) forming belt of fire. 1 gun was placed at N.11.D.70.65 for anti aircraft work. gun emplacements were made in shell holes and shelters were made for the teams. The positions were covered with camouflaged netting. An average of 3000 rounds were fired per night on tracks used by the enemy. The aircraft gun fired on average of 200 rounds per day.	C.O.
	27/5/17		The Brigade was relieved by the night of the 28/5/17 & but the Company remained in the line coming under the orders of the 111th Brigade.	C.O.
	28/5/17			C.O.

WAR DIARY
or
INTELLIGENCE SUMMARY.

Army Form C. 2118.

W. Whitehead

Place	Date	Hour	Summary of Events and Information	Remarks and references to Appendices
TILLOY	29/5/17	6.0 p.m.	11 guns of the company were relieved by 111 M.G.C. 5 guns remain in the front line defence system north of the CAMBRAI Rd.	01
	30/5/17		1 gun was moved from O7B73 to the barricade in TOOL TRENCH at O8D18, this gun was used to assist in the attack on HOOK TRENCH by firing enfilade fire up LONG TRENCH	01
		11.30 p.m.	The 86th Brigade of the 29th Division assisted by the 8th East Lancs of the 112th Brigade attacked HOOK TRENCH, after a very heavy bombardment of the enemy's lines, the enemy soon put up a heavy barrage and the 8th East Lancs entered HOOK TRENCH but were driven out by an enemy counter attack, down HOOK TRENCH from the north. During the attack and counter attack our gun at the barricade fired 1500 rounds and 2 guns at O7B43 assisted in the barrage firing 5000 rounds on the enemy machine gun barrage.	
	31/5/17		Very little hostile activity.	
		6.0 p.m.	The 5 guns were relieved by 111th Brigade and returned to ARRAS. During the term of duty in the trenches we had the following casualties: 3 O.R. wounded, 1 officer slightly wounded.	01

2/Lieut W.V. BAKER

WAR DIARY
INTELLIGENCE SUMMARY

Army Form C. 2118.

Wodafiend

Place	Date	Hour	Summary of Events and Information	Remarks and references to Appendices
TILLOY			During the month the following decorations were received for gallantry in the field. MILITARY MEDAL 4969 Cpl (now Sgt) A. BURROWS } MONCHY 9/4/17 6065 LCpl (wounded) L. HALL } 14/4/17 42740 Pte (now L/Cpl) J. WHEELAN 60989 LCpl (now Cpl) W.W. LIVERMORE 6124 Sgt (wounded) A. PENNINGTON } GREENLAND HILL 23/4/17 5925 Cpl (wounded) A. WESTBURY } 30/4/17	C.O.

SECRET
Vol 16

War Diary
of
11th Machine Gun Company

1st of June 1917 to 30th of June 1917

VOLUME XIX

Subject
To/
H.Q
112th Inf Bde.

Orderly Room — No. MG/106/M — Date 30/6/17 — 112 Machine Gun Co.

Please receive

WAR DIARY of

112th MACHINE GUN COMPANY

for JUNE 1917.

In the field
30/6/17

T. B. Merrick. Lieut for
_____ O.C.
No. 112 M. GUN COMPANY.

WARDIARY
or
INTELLIGENCE SUMMARY.

(Erase heading not required.)

Army Form C. 2118.

Gauntlett Major
No. 112 M.G. Company.

Place	Date	Hour	Summary of Events and Information	Remarks and references to Appendices
ARRAS	1.6.17	2pm	No. 1 & 2 sections marched to AGNES LES DUISANS	
AGNES-LES-DUISANS	2.6.17		Day spent in cleaning up. Kit inspections & readjusting of sections personnel	
	3.6.17	5.30pm	Coy moved into billets at IZEL-LES-HAMEL Lieut DURRANT BH proceeded to U.K. on leave	
	4.6.17		In billets & usual program of work. Informed that No. 43048 L/Cpl S BURGESS (keed'vacter) had been awarded the Military Medal for gallantry during the period 23/30 April 1917	
	5.6.17		Usual work	
	6.6.17		Coy took part in a Brigade Field Day	
	7.6.17 5.0am		Moved to billets in MONNEVILLE	
MONNEVILLE	8.6.17		Marched to DEZELETTE'S training area 1st Army training area	
	9.6.17		Usual work. Coy Drill, Gunfire, mechanism, I.A. etc.	
	10.6.17 9.00am		Church Parades	
DEZELETTES	11.6.17		Major Gauntlett resumes command of the Company on from today and Lieut W Cowie resumes duties of second in command. Extract from the "London Gazette" of the list of "Mentions in Despatches" published 14th May	

No 6033 Sgt WHITE C.Q. 112 M.G.C.

Army Form C. 2118.

WAR DIARY
or
INTELLIGENCE SUMMARY.

No. 112 M. GUN COMPANY.

(Erase heading not required.)

Instructions regarding War Diaries and Intelligence Summaries are contained in F. S. Regs., Part II. and the Staff Manual respectively. Title pages will be prepared in manuscript.

Place	Date	Hour	Summary of Events and Information	Remarks and references to Appendices
DICKEBUSCH	12/6/17 to 16/6/17		Training according to program. The Field Marshal Commander-in-Chief has awarded decorations to the officers and other ranks shewn below for acts of gallantry during operations 7/13 April and 23/30th April. MILITARY CROSS — T/2/Lt W.V.BAKER MILITARY MEDAL — Sergt A.J. CLEGG MILITARY CROSS — LIEUT. T.B. MERRICK	W.J. W.J.
	16/6/17	10.00a	Inspection by G.O.C. 112th Inf Bde	W.J.
	17/6/17 to 19/6/17		Half Company firing revolver + machine gun practices whilst others are ranges (under R.E. Approval) and practices barrage + overhead fire.	W.J.
	20/21 /22		Usual work + Pack-saddle Limbers nearly ready for move to 2nd Army	
	23.6.17	5.a.m	Marched to BOESEGHEM.	T.B.M.
BOESEGHEM	24.6.17	10.a.m	Marched to LA BREARDE.	T.B.M.
LA BREARDE	25.6.17	10a.m.	Marched to LOCRE.	T.B.M.

Army Form C. 2118.

WAR DIARY
or
INTELLIGENCE SUMMARY.
(Erase heading not required.)

Kenn Twoshny
No. 112 M. GUN COMPANY.

Instructions regarding War Diaries and Intelligence Summaries are contained in F. S. Regs., Part II. and the Staff Manual respectively. Title pages will be prepared in manuscript.

Place	Date	Hour	Summary of Events and Information	Remarks and references to Appendices
LOCRE	26.6.17		Day spent in cleaning up	T.B.W.
	27.6.17		Usual programme of work.	T.B.W.
	28.6.17	11 a.m.	Inspection by Army Commander.	T.B.W.
	29.6.17		C.O., section officers, & N.C.O's attended demonstration of tanks in attack at 2nd Army School of Musketry.	T.B.W.
			Company marched to KEMMEL	T.B.W.
KEMMEL	30.6.17.		Work according to programme	T.B.W.

A 5834 Wt. W4973 M687 750,000 8/16 D. D. & L. Ltd. Forms/C.2118/13.

(SECRET)

WAR DIARY

of

112TH MACHINE GUN COMPANY

1ST of JULY 1917 to 31ST of JULY 1917

(VOLUME XVII)

WAR DIARY or INTELLIGENCE SUMMARY

Army Form C. 2118.

No. 112 M.G. COMPANY

Place	Date	Hour	Summary of Events and Information	Remarks and references to Appendices
KEMMEL	1/7/17	10 a.m.	Marched to DRANOUTRE. Brigade now in reserve.	
DRANOUTRE	2/7/17		Morning — improving billets. Afternoon — recreation	
	3/4/5		Training according to programme	
	6/7/17		Nos. 3 and 4 sections on anti-aircraft duty; No. 4 section protecting Divisional HQRS. west of DRANOUTRE, and No. 3 section protecting the village of DRANOUTRE. Scheme for protecting infantry camps & dumps in district arranged by O.C. Coy. and approved by Division.	
	7/8/9		Training according to programme.	
	10/7/17		Marched to DONEGAL FARM — N.31.d.9.7. Ref. Map: France, Sheet 28 S.W. 1/20,000. Brigade now in support.	
	11.7.17		Training	
	12.7.17		Nos. 3 and 4 sections rejoined Coy. from Anti-aircraft duty.	
DONEGAL FARM	13.7.17 14.7.17 15.7.17		Training according to programme. Three guns on anti-aircraft duty.	
	16.7.17		No 1 Section proceeded to forward area to make range emplacements.	

WAR DIARY
or
INTELLIGENCE SUMMARY.

Army Form C. 2118.

No. 11 M.... COMPANY.

Place	Date	Hour	Summary of Events and Information	Remarks and references to Appendices
DONEGAL FARM	16.7.17 / 17.7.17		No 4 section proceeded to Lindenhoek to polish observation balloons against enemy aircraft. No 3 section proceeded to MAYHIEK FARM to make barrage positions	AA&QM
	18.7.17		Training according to programme	AA&QM
	19.7.17		Preparing for the line. No 4 section into forward area to relieve No 1 section	AA&QM
BULLY BEEF FARM	20.7.17		Marched to BULLY BEEF FARM N.26.c.1.9 Ref. Map. FRANCE Sheet 28 S.W. 1/20,000. All guns placed in barrage and defence positions in forward area	AA&QM
	21.7.17		During night of 21.7.17. Harassing was carried out. Emplacements dug and improved.	AA&QM
FARM	22.7.17		4 guns fired from 7 pm to 7 am assisting a raid by brigade on our left. 5000 rounds were fired. Two O.R. wounded during this day.	AA&QM
	23.7.17		All guns fired barrage fire to support raid by 10th L.N. Lancs at 7 a.m. 80,000 rounds were fired. One O.R. wounded during the day. Enemy aircraft were engaged during the early morning	AA&QM
	24.7.17		During night 23/24 10,000 rounds were fired on RIFLE and BAR FARMS. Harassing fire was also carried out on selected targets. 2,000 rounds being fired on the. One O.R. was wounded during the day. Emplacements improved and enlarged. Work done engaged during the day.	AA&QM

Army Form C. 2118.

WAR DIARY
or
INTELLIGENCE SUMMARY.

(Erase heading not required.)

112 M. G. COMPANY

Place	Date	Hour	Summary of Events and Information	Remarks and references to Appendices
BULLY BEEF FARM.	25.7.17		During tonight selected targets were fired on by all guns. Enemy aircraft was engaged in the early morning. 2nd Lieut. A.V. Haden was wounded also one O.R.	O.C.M
TYRONE FARM	26.7.17		Eight of the company were relieved on night 25/26 by 111 M.G. Coy. 3000 rounds were fired by remaining guns on selected targets. The relieved half of the Coy. together with C.H.Q. and Transport moved to TYRONE FARM, BRANOUTRE.	O.C.M
	27.7.17		Harassing fire on selected target. Enemy aircraft engaged.	C.O.M
	28.7.17		Harassing fire on selected target. One O.R. was killed during the day. During night 28/29 all damage positions were completed.	O.C.M
	29.7.17		Remaining eight guns relieved by 63rd M.G. Coy.	
	30.7.17		Company moved into forward area and took up its special barrage position.	O.C.M
	31.7.17		Barrage was opened at 3.50 a.m. covering advance of the infantry. At 7.50 am another barrage was given for second phase of the advance. Harassing fire was kept up during the day. In conjunction with artillery. During the day 200,000 rounds were fired.	O.C.M

War Diary
18/12th M.G. Coy
Aug 1917

SECRET

WAR DIARY
of
112th MACHINE GUN COMPANY.
1st of AUGUST 1917 to 31st of AUGUST 1917

(VOLUME XVIII)

Army Form C. 2118.

WAR DIARY
or
INTELLIGENCE SUMMARY.
(Erase heading not required.)

No. 112 M. GUN COMPANY

Place	Date	Hour	Summary of Events and Information	Remarks and references to Appendices
TYRONNE FARM	1.8.17		Harassing fire carried out on the enemy.	APPW.
DRANOUTRE	2.8.17		Harassing fire carried out on the enemy	APPW.
	3.8.17		Harassing fire carried out on the enemy. Coy relieved on the night of the 3/4, by the 111th M.G. Coy. The Coy. returned to TYRONNE FARM, DRANOUTRE.	APPW.
	4.8.17		Day was spent in cleaning of guns, equipment etc.	APPW.
	5.8.17		Sunday: Coy attended church parade	APPW.
LA POLKA, KEMMEL.	6.8.17		Coy. moved to DOCTOR'S HOUSE, LA POLKA, KEMMEL. The 112th Bde. was then in support.	APPW.
	7.8.17		MAJOR D.B. CALDER arrived and command of the Coy. on this day. Officers reconnoitred the line, prior to relieving 157 comp. M.G.C.	APPW.
	8.8.17		Coy. relieved 157 + 158 Coy. M.G.C.	APPW.
KEMMEL CHATEAU.	9.8.17		MAJOR H.G. GAUNTLETT proceeded to England. Rear H.Q. moved to KEMMEL CHATEAU. The Coy. in the line improved emplacements dug outs etc & collected salvage. Harassing fire carried out on the enemy during the night.	APPW.

Army Form C. 2118.

David Morris Major

No. 112 M. GUN COMPANY

WAR DIARY
or
INTELLIGENCE SUMMARY.
(Erase heading not required.)

Instructions regarding War Diaries and Intelligence Summaries are contained in F.S. Regs., Part II. and the Staff Manual respectively. Title pages will be prepared in manuscript.

Place	Date	Hour	Summary of Events and Information	Remarks and references to Appendices
KEMMEL CHATEAU	10.8.17		In the early morning covering fire was carried out to assist the division on our right. 12,000 rounds were fired.	O.C.M.G.
	11.8.17		In the early morning between 3 am and 5 am, indirect fire was carried out on CENTRE FARM (O.18 c 40.15.) FRANCE SHEET 28 S.W.) at the regret of the Infantry. The gun pits and emplacements were improved.	O.C.M.G.
	12.8.17		Indirect fire was carried out on six selecting targets. 4,500 rounds were fired. One O.R. was wounded by shell fire.	O.C.M.G.
	13.8.17		During day and night indirect fire was carried out on nine targets. 16,750 rounds were fired. Two O.R. were wounded by shell fire.	O.C.M.G.
	14.8.17		On conjunction with heavy Howitzers and by arrangement with D.M.G.O., 15,000 rounds were fired at arranged hours on farm buildings, tracks etc in (front of) the WARNETON LINE.	O.C.M.G.
	15.8.17		Indirect fire was kept up at intervals by day and night on farms, tracts, suspected H.Q.s etc in enemy front	O.C.M.G.

WAR DIARY
or
INTELLIGENCE SUMMARY.
(Erase heading not required.)

Army Form C. 2118.

David Powell
O.C.
No. 112 M. GUN COMPANY

Place	Date	Hour	Summary of Events and Information	Remarks and references to Appendices
KEMMEL CHATEAU	16.8.17		During today indirect fire was carried out on the same targets as the previous day. At night 16/17 the Coy was relieved by 63rd and 247th Coys. M.G.C. After relief Coy returned to KEMMEL CHATEAU. Three O.R. were wounded by shell fire.	Coy
	17.8.17 to 21.8.17		Coy in rest at KEMMEL CHATEAU	WT
	22.8.17		Preparation for line lectures given by Divisional Commander on the "Braunne System of defence"	WT
		5.0 pm	Coy paraded and marched up to the line to relieve 8 guns of 63rd Coy M.G.C. and 8 guns of 247 Coy M.G.C.	WT
		11.30 pm	Relief Complete	
	23.8.17		Anti-aircraft guns fired 7,250 rounds on enemy aeroplanes. Indirect fire in conjunction with artillery on selected targets — Rounds fired 19,000. Collection of salvage. Improvement of dug outs and emplacements. Erection of A.A. mountings of New Dug Out at Coy H.O.	

Army Form C. 2118.

WAR DIARY
or
INTELLIGENCE SUMMARY.
(Erase heading not required.)

D.W. Roach O.C.
No. 112 M. GUN COMPANY.

Place	Date	Hour	Summary of Events and Information	Remarks and references to Appendices
	24/8/17		Indirect fire by day and night in conjunction with bombardment by artillery on 14 targets. No. of rounds fired 28,250	WT
	25/8/17		Construction of new emplacements shelters etc. Salvage collected. Enemy aircraft was fired on during the morning and was driven off. Tracer ammunition was of great assistance. Indirect fire on Enemy points of movement dumps etc. Salvage collected. Repair of trenches. Two shelters erected for ROSEWOOD gun teams.	WT
	26/8/17		Usual indirect fire. 20,450 rounds fired. 4,000 rounds fired on SOS signal being given. 250 rounds on E.A. Trenches dug out, and positions improved.	WT
	27/8/17		In conjunction with raid by 11th R. War R. 36000 rounds were fired on fixed barrage. 21,500 rounds fired on other targets given by R/W.Q.	WT
KEMMEL (le Chateau)	28/8/17 29.A. 4-30 A.		Company relieved by 111th Coy M/C KEMMEL In billets at Le Chateau	WT

A.5834 Wt.W4973 M687 730.000 8/16 D.D.&L.Ltd. Forms/C.2118/13.

Army Form C. 2118.

WAR DIARY
or
INTELLIGENCE SUMMARY.

(Erase heading not required.)

David Baird O.C.

No. 112 M. GUN COMPANY.

Place	Date	Hour	Summary of Events and Information	Remarks and references to Appendices
KEMMEL	31/8/17		Inspection by Brig. Gen. A.E. IRVINE, G.O.C. 112th Bde. The Coy was congratulated on its smart turn out, and on the good work it had carried out, when lack in the line viz in connection with Raid carried out on morning of 27th inst, and in the carrying out of the "Rockers" S.O.S. on 26th inst.	W.S.

WAR DIARY
of
1st MACHINE GUN COMPANY

1st SEPTEMBER to 30 SEPTEMBER 1917

Vol 19

Volume XIX

Subject

To/
112th Inf Bde

Please find herewith
WAR DIARY for the month
of September 1917.
112th MACHINE GUN COMPANY
please

Inkefield
1/10/17

David B Calder Major
———————— O.C.
No. 112 M. GUN COMPANY.

Army Form C. 2118.

No. 112 M. GUN COMPANY.

WAR DIARY
or
INTELLIGENCE SUMMARY.
(Erase heading not required.)

Instructions regarding War Diaries and Intelligence Summaries are contained in F. S. Regs., Part II. and the Staff Manual respectively. Title pages will be prepared in manuscript.

Place	Date	Hour	Summary of Events and Information	Remarks and references to Appendices
IN CAMP NEAR SIEGE FARM	1/9/17 & 2/9/17		Company in Reserve billets. O.C. Coy and 2nd I/C reconnoitred the line, with view to the relief on the 3/4 inst. The 112th Inf.Bde relieved 116th Inf.Bde and 17th Inf.Bde (one battalion only) from YPRES - COMINES canal (inclusive) to J31 a 75.75 on nights of 2/3 and 3/4.	WJ
	3.9.17		Company made preparations for the line and relieved the 16th M.G.C. (13 guns) and the 17th Coy M.G.C. (3 guns) on the night 3/4 inst.	WJ
	4.9.17		Anti-aircraft guns fired 650 rounds during morning on enemy aeroplane. Much work was done in improvement of emplacements and dug-outs, building of latrines and erection of a.a. mountings.	WJ
	5.9.17		E.A. engaged by our M.Guns, when within range, and on each occasion returned to their own lines. At 8.30 am, one plane appeared to be hit by several "Tracer" Bullets. 4,130 rounds were fired.	WJ
	6.9.17		E.A. driven away from CATERPILLAR by M.G fire. Rounds fired 2,400. Harassing fire was carried out during night 5/6 on following targets CROSS ROADS P.8a 65.10 CLAY FARM P1a 50 75 MOAT FARM P.11b 80 8 PIONEER FARM P1a 50 75	1/100.00 HOLLEBEKE
	7.9.17		250 Rounds fired on E.A. which immediately returned to its own lines. One new emplacement built. Trenches and dug outs improved	WJ
	8.9.17		Harassing fire on following points. MAY FARM P1d.40.90 WOOD FARM J31d 50 20 Rounds fired 7,500. Two new emplacements made. An officer of the Royal Trailers was sent this morning to Rlg. SQ. & a report been forwarded to Rdr. SQ.	WJ
	9.9.17		Usual firing. EA much shelling collected and emplacement improved. He evidently does and a	LM

A5834 Wt.W4973 M687 750,000 8/16 D.D. & L. Ltd. Forms/C.2118/13.

WAR DIARY
or
INTELLIGENCE SUMMARY.
(Erase heading not required.)

Army Form C. 2118.

David Blaikie Major

Place	Date	Hour	Summary of Events and Information	Remarks and references to Appendices
	10.9.17		Much artillery activity. 500 rounds fired at E.A. a big fire was seen at 2.20pm in front of WERVICQ CH lasting for 40 minutes. Our M.Guns opened a barrage at 8.40pm in response to SOS but no artillery fire ceased after two minutes, our guns stopped	W.J
	11.9.17		E.A. very active. 480 rounds fired, one 3 E.A. driven off. Tracer bullets found to be very useful for this kind of work. On one attempted raid by the 6th Bedford Regt 15,250 rounds in conjunction with (commanded by LT. T.B MERRICK MC) put were fired. Two guns in the front line on either flank two other guns in the up a fixed band of flanking fire Other 8 guns of the Coy put up front fired at suspected hostile M.G.'s. received from B.O.L. CAMPION (DSO) a box barrage. A congratulatory message was also stating that C.O. 6th Bedford's thanking us for good work done, he silenced a hostile machine gun	W.J
	12.9.17 13.9.17		Officers of 57 & 58 Corp M.G.C. Came up the line to arrange relief. The Coy was relieved on the night 12/13 and returned to Camp near SIEGE FARM.	
WESTOUTRE	14.9.17		March to Camp at 13.6.8.9. near WESTOUTRE	W.J
	15.9.17		Baths at ST JANS CAPELLE. Rest of day spent in a general clean up, Kit - inspection, and paying out.	W.J
	16.9.17		Church Parades. Football tournament commenced	W.J
	17.9.17			
	18.9.17		Usual parades and taking of the Barrowes open officer.	W.J

WAR DIARY or INTELLIGENCE SUMMARY

Army Form C. 2118.

Dawn/Balder Maj

Instructions regarding War Diaries and Intelligence Summaries are contained in F. S. Regs., Part II. and the Staff Manual respectively. Title pages will be prepared in manuscript.

(Erase heading not required.)

Place	Date	Hour	Summary of Events and Information	Remarks and references to Appendices
	19/9/17	8.0pm	Company moved to CHEAPSIDE (in Bde reserve to 19th Div) coming under his divn notice for action from dawn the following morning.	
	20/9/17		Remained in bivouac all day.	
	21/9/17	2.30pm	Coy ordered to move back to WESTOUTRE at 5.0pm. There was ordered to 6.30pm.	
			Moved to WESTOUTRE.	
	22/9/17	9.15am	Coy ordered for the line to relieve 118th Bn Regt. Remaining Coy joined CO at advance brushing moved off.	
			After remainder the Coy an arrived at 6.0pm and the C.O. at BUS HOUSE where an hour after was unlimbered and the bivouacy tested since 3am.	
	23/9/17	5.00am	Spun tot was unlimbered when they moved up to complete relief. Relief complete. 3 O.R wounded. SHREWSBURY FOREST SECTOR taken over.	
		9.0am		
		2.0pm	Artillery carries out practice barrage.	
		4.40pm		
	24/9/17		Enemy shewed whole brigade area nearly all day in reply to our frequent artillery barrages. 2/Lt HUGGILL wounded. Two O.R. killed and 2 O.R. wounded.	
	25/9/17	5.30am	1 O.R. Killed + 1 O.R. wounded at Bn/H.Q. 1 O.R. missing. 1 O.R. wounded } all by shell fire	

Army Form C. 2118.

WAR DIARY
or
INTELLIGENCE SUMMARY.
(Erase heading not required.)

David Halter Major

Place	Date	Hour	Summary of Events and Information	Remarks and references to Appendices
IN FRONT EVERY FOREST EAST	31/8/17	5.5.0 pm 3.0 am	On our left attacked, and also Division of X Corps further North. On Division being on our left no operations in M/g barrage on back. Guns firing 19,000 rounds. 2 O.R. wounded. Practice Artillery Barrage by IX Corps Heavies.	
	1/9/17		2 O.R. Recd. 3 O.R. wounded. 2 O.R. wounded but remained at duty.	
	2/9/17	6 Mon 5.0 am	Boy was relieved by 57 boy m/g - Crimency. Brown met boy coming out and took in to Div. Reliw. was not completed until about Noon owing to one section of relieving boy being shelled on its way in and having near all its men in casualties. Enemy shim em in the Coy. casualties occurred in the following. 1 Officer killed 5 O.R. 1 Officer wounded 17 O.R. wounded 1 O.R. Missing (2 remained at duty)	

A5834 Wt. W4973 M687 750,000 8/16 D. D. & L. Ltd. Forms/C.2118/13.

Army Form C. 2118.

WAR DIARY
or
INTELLIGENCE SUMMARY.
(Erase heading not required.)

Dun Blauden Map

Instructions regarding War Diaries and Intelligence Summaries are contained in F. S. Regs., Part II. and the Staff Manual respectively. Title pages will be prepared in manuscript.

Place	Date	Hour	Summary of Events and Information	Remarks and references to Appendices
	28/9/17		Two guns were completely destroyed by shell fire and three damaged. The boy had a particularly trying time but came out of it very well. 2/Lieut B.H. DURRANT showed great initiative on the 21st when after having his a gun complete destroyed, and the remainder of his having no ammunition he had a German M.G. which he was action by the use of German screws mounted and no hymn rail, slave by the use of German keen in action ammunition	(4) (4)
	29/9/17		The day no rearies in cleaning up, cleaning appearance in equipment and clothing.	(4)
	30/9/17		Church Parade.	

WA 20

WAR DIARY
of
112th MACHINE GUN COMPANY
1st OCTOBER To 31st OCTOBER 1917

(VOLUME XX)

Subject War Diary
To
112th Inf Bde

[Stamp: ORDERLY ROOM No. M6/122/W Date 1/11/17 — 112 MACHINE GUN CO.]

Herewith please find
War Diary of the 112th MACHINE
GUN COY for the month
of October 1917. Vol. 20

In the field
Nov 1st /17

W. Jonks Lieut for O.C.
No. 112 M. GUN COMPANY

WAR DIARY
or
INTELLIGENCE SUMMARY

Army Form C. 2118.

M.O.T. Langton Capt.
O.C.
No. 112 M. GUN COMPANY.

(Erase heading not required.)

Place	Date	Hour	Summary of Events and Information	Remarks and references to Appendices
WILLEBEEK CAMP	1/10/17		Coy lay in support at WILLEBEEK CAMP. Day spent in training.	WJ
	2/10/17		Completed overhauling and cleaning of all kit	WJ
ROF (22.8.17 hours)	3/10/17		Day spent in training. No 2 Section moved into 'line' to reinforce 63rd M.G.C.	
	4/10/17		Under orders to move at 15 minutes notice	WJ
	5/10/17 to 6/10/17		Enemy trying to move and pushed forward for line. No 1, 3 Sections moved up into the line where 112th Infantry Bde. are the	
IN THE LINE			Coy went T.26 d.70 90 to YPRES – MENIN ROAD J.21 b 35.03	WJ
	7th		Coy in response to S.O.S. signal	
	8th		fired in connection with HIW YEOMANS and 8 Div Relief	
	9th		Barrage fire in connection with operations on our North	
	10th		Harassing fire carried on	
	11th		Company relieved by 63rd Coy and withdrew to WILLEBEEK CAMP	
	12th		Day spent in cleaning and checking of kit handed over by 63 M.G.C.	
	13th		Coy moved under Brigade Arrangements to CORUNNA CAMP M.15.C Central	
	14th		Church Parade	
	15		Cleaning and cleaning of arms kit bivouac horses	
	16 17		Training according to Programme	
	18		Coy moved to Frontier Camp	
	22 25		Training of Company at Frontier Programme	WJ

A 5834 Wt.W4973 M687 750,000 8/16 D.D. & L. Ltd. Forms/C.2118/13.

Army Form C. 2118.

O.C.
No. 112 M. GUN COMPANY.

WAR DIARY
or
INTELLIGENCE SUMMARY.

(Erase heading not required.)

Instructions regarding War Diaries and Intelligence Summaries are contained in F. S. Regs., Part II. and the Staff Manual respectively. Title pages will be prepared in manuscript.

Place	Date	Hour	Summary of Events and Information	Remarks and references to Appendices
LOCRE	26/10/17		Company moved to YORK HUTS. LOCRE. Major his been relinquished command of Coy on appointment as DMGO 17th Div. Capt W.H.C.Ramsden approved o/c in succession	WJ
	27th			
	28th		Church parades	WJ
	29th 30th 31st		Training	WJ

Vol 21

CONFIDENTIAL.

WAR DIARY

OF

112th MACHINE GUN COMPANY

FROM 1st NOVEMBER 1917 TO 30th NOVEMBER 1917.

(VOLUME XXI.)

To
O/AD
112th Inf Bde.

Herewith War Diary
for November
112th Machine Gun Company
Nlese

In the field
Nov 30/17

H W S Ramsden 2/Lt
Lieut
O.C.
No. 112 M. GUN COMPANY.

WAR DIARY or INTELLIGENCE SUMMARY

Army Form C. 2118.

No. 112 M. GUN COMPANY.

Place	Date	Hour	Summary of Events and Information	Remarks and references to Appendices
LOCRE	5.11.17		Company in rest billets at LOCRE. Training according to programme	W.D
	6.11.17		Company attended commemoration service of Sunday 6th inst.	W.D
	7.11.17		The Company went on a distance training in the afternoon (march with complete kit and carried off by Bus) (evening – maximum number of miles). The Company was in cadre as the inter-Brigade event and Brigade won 1st prize and Challenge Cup	
			The afternoon was spent in preparing to the line.	
YPRES-COMINES CANAL SECTOR	8.11.17		Company took over 227 Bn M.G Section north of YPRES – COMINES CANAL (squads)	W.D
	9.11.17		Two Vickers guns sent into line and took up positions in BELGIAN WOOD. Harassing fire on selected targets.	W.D
	10.11.17		Two guns in forward group and six guns at Barrage group were relieved by 115th Company M.G.C.	W.D
	11.11.17			
	12.11.17		Two guns withdrawn from BELGIAN WOOD and added to Barrage group making it an eight gun battery instead of a six	W.D
	13/14/15		Harassing fire on selected targets.	
	15.11.17		Eight guns in line were relieved by eight guns from new H.Q. The sector now being held as follows: 115 Coy. Two guns forward group. 112 Coy. Six guns Barrage group. 112nd Coy. Eight guns Barrage group. 112th Company taking over command.	W.D

Army Form C. 2118.

No. 112 M. GUN COMPANY.

WAR DIARY
or
INTELLIGENCE SUMMARY.
(Erase heading not required.)

Instructions regarding War Diaries and Intelligence Summaries are contained in F. S. Regs., Part II. and the Staff Manual respectively. Title pages will be prepared in manuscript.

Place	Date	Hour	Summary of Events and Information	Remarks and references to Appendices
YPRES- COMINES CANAL SECTOR	26/8/17		Harrassing fire on selected targets	W.J.
	27/8/17		Half company being relieved by J company at Ravage group O.C. 112 Company taking over command	W.J.
	22/8/17		Harrassing fire on allotted lines	W.J.
	24/8/17		Left gun from rear Headquarters relieved 11 L.G. in forward and support groups. Eight guns of 111'S Coy relieved our eight guns at Ravage group. O.C. 111'S Coy company taking over command	W.J.
	28/29/30		Harrassing fire	W.J.
			The Coy remained in rear at near Headquarters where engaged in training, also in improving camp and billets	W.J.

WA 22

WAR DIARY
of
112th MACHINE GUN COMPANY
1st of DECEMBER to 31st DECEMBER
1917

(VOLUME XXII)

Subject   War Diary
To/ H.Q.
113th Inf Bde

No. MG/416/1
Date 1/1/18

Please receive
WAR DIARY (Vol XXII
for December 1917
112th MACHINE GUN COMPANY

In the field
1/1/18.

H.H. Gausden
Capt
O.C
No. 112 M. GUN COMPANY.

Army Form C. 2118.

[Signature] W.T. Pemberton(?)
O.C.
No. 112 M. GUN COMPANY.

WAR DIARY
or
INTELLIGENCE SUMMARY.
(Erase heading not required.)

Instructions regarding War Diaries and Intelligence Summaries are contained in F. S. Regs., Part II. and the Staff Manual respectively. Title pages will be prepared in manuscript.

Place	Date	Hour	Summary of Events and Information	Remarks and references to Appendices
SPIEGEL FARM	1.12.17		Nos. 2 and 4 sections in the line. 2 guns of No 2 section were raided by the enemy. Bombs were thrown causing 4 casualties, all O.R. The enemy were driven off. Otherwise all was quiet.	CRBW.
ditto	2.12.17		The this section in support were relieved by 1+3 sections. The O.C. of this Coy. took over command of left sector M.G's of the divisional front. Enemy fire was maintained on the enemy from HALF-WAY-HOUSE.	CRBW
ditto	3.12.17		No 6. gun - in support group - fired on an enemy working party at J.27.a.3.4. dispersing it. Otherwise the day was quiet.	CRBW
ditto	4.12.17		Enemy shelled our guns at JULES FARM without causing damage. Otherwise nothing to report.	CRBW
ditto	5.12.17		No. 6. sniping gun - in the afternoon fired on a party of the enemy south of BEREY COTS dispersing it. The enemy shelled IMAGE TRENCH heavily with 4.2 for 3 hours during the night, Probably searching for our guns. Enemy's machine guns harassed COKE'S COTTAGE.	CRBW.
ditto	6.12.17		Sniper No. 7+8 at HALF-WAY-HOUSE, engaged a target at ALACRA HOUSES, firing in all 1000 rounds at intervals.	CRBW
ditto	7.12.17		Harassing fire was carried out from HALF-WAY-HOUSE, but nothing of importance happened on our front.	CRBW.
ditto	8.12.17		Nos. 1+3 section in SUPPORT AREA were relieved by 2 sections of 111 Coy. M.G.C. Nos. 2 and 4 sections of this Coy. & section of 111 Coy. at the BARRAGE POSITION. The O.C. of this Coy. handed over command of left sector M.G's to O.C. of 111 Coy.	CRBW.
ditto	9.12.17 to		One section in BARRAGE POSITION kept up harassing fire on enemy's underposts.	CRBW
ditto	15.12.17		30,000 rounds were fired during this period. The enemy artillery was not very active.	CRBW

A534 Wt.W4974/M687 750,000 8/16 D.D. & L. Ltd. Forms/C.2118/13

Army Form C. 2118.

WAR DIARY
or
INTELLIGENCE SUMMARY.
(Erase heading not required.)

No. 112 M. GUN COMPANY.

Place	Date	Hour	Summary of Events and Information	Remarks and references to Appendices
SEIGE FARM	15.12.17		Nos. 113 Section of this Coy relieved 2/4 Section at BARRAGE POSITION to the C.O. of this Coy relieved Co. 111th Coy. Harassing fire was maintained during the night.	OBBW.
ditto	16.12.17 & 17.12.17		It was expected the enemy were relieving on the night of the 16/17.12.17. Heavy fire was maintained on enemy's tracks, and harassing fire was placed on enemy's centers of movement. 22,000 rounds being fired in all.	CBBW.
ditto	18.12.17		In accordance with orders from D.M.G.O. to co-operate with artillery in a dummy raid against GAME COPSE. Machine Guns fired 23,000 rounds. Shortly fire was opened the enemy put up 12 very lights. On the morning of this day enemy aircraft was engaged, 500 rounds being fired. One plane was seen to fall but control was regained. The neighbourhood of PACIC FARM. In the afternoon a further 500 rounds were fired at his artillery emplacements. They were driven off. During the night 18/19.12.17 Harassing fire was maintained on two specially selected targets.	CBBW.
ditto	19.12.17		On the evening of 19/20.12.17 in accordance with instructions from D.M.G.O. to co-operate with artillery in another dummy raid against GAME COPSE 26,500 rounds were fired. The following casualties occurred 1 O.R. killed 4 O.R. wounded	CBBW.
ditto	20.12.17		Just after midday on instructions received from H.Q. 111th I.J. Bde. 2000 rounds by the 8 guns in BARRAGE POSITION in V.O.S. Line. On the night 20/21.12.17 Harassing fire was maintained on specially selected targets.	CBBW.
ditto	21.12.17		Harassing fire was maintained at irregular intervals during the day.	CBBW.

Army Form C. 2118.

M. Tamplin O.C.
No. 112 M. GUN COMPANY.

WAR DIARY
or
INTELLIGENCE SUMMARY.
(Erase heading not required.)

Instructions regarding War Diaries and Intelligence Summaries are contained in F. S. Regs., Part II. and the Staff Manual respectively. Title pages will be prepared in manuscript.

Place	Date	Hour	Summary of Events and Information	Remarks and references to Appendices
SEIGE FARM	22/12/17		C.O. 111th Coy. relieved C.O. of this Coy. in the line. Two sections of the 111th relieved Nos. 1 & 3 sections of this Coy. in BARRAGE POSITION. Nos. 2 & 4 sections relieved 2 section of the 111th Coy. in the SUPPORT AREA. Owing to very good observation, the relief to the weather, the enemy apparently observed the relief when No. 2&4 section reached the GLEN. The enemy shelled the place heavily with field guns causing the following casualties: 3 O.R. killed.	CRBW
ditto	23/12/17		No firing was carried out from SUPPORT AREA. The day was quiet.	CRBW
ditto	24/12/17		Enemy field guns were very active in the support area. He bombarded our position at JAVA TRENCH, causing no casualties.	CRBW
ditto	25/12/17		At dawn observation was very good. Our sniping guns at the CUTTING and JULES FARM dispersed several parties of the enemy during the morning to supply gun at JULES FARM engaged EAST FARM, killing one of the enemy. During the night the enemy was very active with field guns. The half Coy. at R.H.Q. held X was festivities. A very enjoyable evening was spent.	CRBW
ditto	26/12/17 & 27/12/17		Harassing was carried out from HALF-WAY HOUSE. On the 27th inst., 2 guns of the 111th Coy. moved up from BARRAGE position to HALF-WAY HOUSE. From this date the guns at this position came under the command of O.C. BARRAGE GROUP.	CRBW

Army Form C. 2118.

O.C.
No. 112 M. GUN COMPANY.

WAR DIARY
or
INTELLIGENCE SUMMARY.
(Erase heading not required.)

Instructions regarding War Diaries and Intelligence Summaries are contained in F. S. Regs., Part II. and the Staff Manual respectively. Title pages will be prepared in manuscript.

Place	Date	Hour	Summary of Events and Information	Remarks and references to Appendices
SEIGE FARM	28.12.17		The C.O. of this Coy. returned. C.O. 111th in the line 2 1/4 sections in the PUPPORT AREA were relieved by 112 section. The relief was carried out without Cas.	CREAN
ditto	29.12.17		6. the night 28/29th harassing fire was carried on. BERRY COTTS.- HALF WAY HOUSE; 5000 rounds were fired. Casualties; 1 O.R. killed.	CREAN
ditto	30.12.17		In the early harassing fire was maintained on selected targets.	CREAN
ditto	31.12.17		6 the night 30/31 harassing fire was maintained at irregular intervals. An enemy relief was suspected. 6000 rounds were fired. Casualties 1 O.R. killed.	CREAN

WAR DIARY
or
INTELLIGENCE SUMMARY.

(Erase heading not required.)

Army Form C. 2118.

No. 112 M. GUN Co.

Place	Date	Hour	Summary of Events and Information	Remarks and references to Appendices
SIEGE FARM	1.1.18		Capt. RAMSDEN in command. 1 LEFT SECTOR M.G.C. 1 & 3 section in the line. Harassing fire was maintained, which was intensified at certain periods on LONE, KENT, SWAGGER and END FARMS, and also battery H.Q. T3 & d and area surrounding. 37,000 rounds were fired. An enemy party, about 10 strong, were observed at Brownville Cab. Stand. fired & and dispersed.	APPEN
ditto	2.1.18		Harassing fire carried out with all guns. An enemy party was observed by firing gun at JULES FARM. The party was dispersed, no man appeared to be hit. 12,500 rounds were fired during the day.	APPEN
ditto	3.1.18		Harassing fire was carried out and enemy party dispersed by sniping guns. 14,000 rounds were fired in all.	APPEN
ditto	4.1.18		O.C. 111 Coy. M.G.C. took over command of L.S.M 48 for Capt. RAMSDEN. 2 & 4 section Ohio Coy and 2 section of 111 Coy relieved 18 guns in the line. The usual Harassing fire was carried out. 20,000 rounds were fired.	APPEN
ditto	5.1.18		Nothing of importance. Usual harassing carried out. 30,000 rounds were fired.	APPEN
ditto	6.1.18		30,000 rounds were fired on enemy tracks, trenches etc. No an enemy relief was reported.	APPEN
ditto	7.1.18		Usual harassing fire maintained during the night. 25,000 rounds were fired.	APPEN
ditto	8.1.18		35,000 rounds were fired on enemy tracks etc. Suspected enemy relief.	APPEN

WAR DIARY
or
INTELLIGENCE SUMMARY.

Army Form C. 2118.

No. 112 M. GUN COMPANY

Place	Date	Hour	Summary of Events and Information	Remarks and references to Appendices
SIEGE FARM	9.1.18		On the night of 9/10 the 111th Inf. Bde carried out two raids, one by R.B's and other by K.R.R.C. Machine guns gave valuable assistance. This Coy. provided 8 guns for barrage fire — 6 at BARRAGE GROUP and 2 at HALF WAY HOUSE. One gun of this Coy. with picked team, in addition to above eight guns, gave direct covering fire for the two raids from BITTER W.6.D.	CRPW
ditto	10.1.18		The TRANSPORT of this Coy. moved at 8.30 a.m. for rest area. GENERAL BIRDWOOD Cmdg. AUSTRALIANS in FRANCE, congratulated the TRANSPORT Officer, 2/Lieut. A.J. PURVES on the turn out of his Coy. transport and enquiring what Army it was. On the night of 10/11/1.18 staged through at BRADELLE C. On the same night the 4th Australian M.G. Coy. relieved the 2 section of 112 Coy M.G.C. and 2 section 111 Coy. M.G.C. in the line.	CRPW
LYNDE	11.1.18		TRANSPORT proceeded to LYNDE in BLARINGHEM area, arriving shortly before noon. The Coy. proceeded by train from DICKEBUSCH, the entraining at ERBLICHEM marching from Renee to WEBBS ast LYNDE arriving about 2 pm.	CRBW
ditto	12.1.18 to 14.1.18		Three days spent in cleaning up and checking hit etc. together with usual Coy. Training. The afternoons were spent in recreation.	CRPS
ditto	15.1.18		A letter was received from GENERAL BIRDWOOD, AUSTRALIANS, through the usual channels congratulating the Commanding Officer on the excellent condition of his Coy. Training were carried out.	CRPW

Army Form C. 2118.

No. 112 M. GUN COMP.

WAR DIARY
or
INTELLIGENCE SUMMARY.
(Erase heading not required.)

Instructions regarding War Diaries and Intelligence Summaries are contained in F. S. Regs., Part II. and the Staff Manual respectively. Title pages will be prepared in manuscript.

Place	Date	Hour	Summary of Events and Information	Remarks and references to Appendices
LYNDE	16.1.18 & 17.1.18		Both days spent in usual Coy. training.	
ditto	18.1.18		Capt. W.H.C. RAMSDEN proceeded on leave to United Kingdom. Lieut. C. PALMER assumed command of the Coy. Usual Coy. training carried out.	
ditto	19.1.18 to 21.1.18		Three days spent in usual Coy. training.	
ditto	22.1.18 & 23.1.18		Inspection of mobilization equipment by D.A.D.O.S.	
RENESCURE	24.1.18		This Coy. interchanged billets with 63 Coy. M.G.C. in RENESCURE AREA	
ditto	25.1.18		Inspection of mobilization equipment completed by DADOS.	
ditto	26.1.18 to 31.1.18		Coy. training was proceeded with.	

(IR 24

Confidential.

War Diary

of

112th Company M.G.C.

From 1st February 1918 to 28th February 1918.

(Volume XXIV)

WAR DIARY or INTELLIGENCE SUMMARY

Army Form C. 2118.

No. 112 M. GUN COMPANY

(Erase heading not required.)

Place	Date	Hour	Summary of Events and Information	Remarks and references to Appendices
EBLINGHEM	1.2.18		Coy. in rest in EBLINGHEM area	4838w
	2.2.18		Coy. training was ~~practically~~ carried out.	4838w
"	3.2.18		CAPT. W.H.C. RAMSDEN rejoined from leave to U.K. and took over command of the Coy. from LIEUT. C. PALMER.	4838w
"	4.2.18 to 10.2.18		These days spent in Coy. training	4838w
"	11.2.18		Inter-section competition was held in the morning. Sports in the afternoon and in the evening a concert was held.	4838w
"	12.2.18		This day spent in Coy. training	4838w
"	13.2.18		Transport moved by road to LA CLYTTE morning off at 8.30 a.m. and stopping the night at STRAZEELE	4838w
LA CLYTTE CAMP	14.2.18		CAPT W.H.C RAMSDEN proceeded on course to G.H.Q. School. LIEUT. C. PALMER assumed command of the Coy. The Coy. moved by rail from EBLINGHEM to DICKEBUSCH and from there by road to LA CLYTTE CAMP. Transport arrived about 1 p.m.	4839w
"	15.2.18		The Coy relieved the 66th Coy. M.G.C. in the line on the night 15/16	4838w
MAIDA CAMP (CAFE BELGE)	16.2.18		Rear HQ moved by road from LA CLYTTE CAMP to MAIDA CAMP (CAFE BELGE).	4838w
	17.2.18		The Coy. carried out harassing fire on various targets in the enemy line, including MENIN ROAD. 6,000 rounds were fired.	4838w
"	18.2.18		Usual harassing fire carried out throughout night.	4838w
"	19.2.18		Harassing carried on. Pin tanks (centres?) movement etc. at intervals during fortnight	4838w
FORESTER CAMP	20.2.18		111 Coy. M.G.C. relieved 112 Coy. M.G.C. in relieve in the night 20/21. The Coy. in relief returned to FORESTER CAMP.	4838w
"	21.2.18 to 25.2.18		These days spent ... Coy training	4838w

C. Palmer Lt.
Coy.

Army Form C. 2118.

C. Delure/t
a/ No. 112 M. GUN COMPANY

WAR DIARY
or
INTELLIGENCE SUMMARY.

(Erase heading not required.)

Instructions regarding War Diaries and Intelligence Summaries are contained in F. S. Regs., Part II. and the Staff Manual respectively. Title pages will be prepared in manuscript.

Place	Date	Hour	Summary of Events and Information	Remarks and references to Appendices
MAIDA CAMP (CAFÉ BELGE)	26.2.18		The Coy. relieved the 111th Coy. in the line. Rear H.Q. moved from FORESTER CAMP to MAIDA CAMP (CAFÉ BELGE)	O.R.P.W
	27.2.18		Harassing fire carried out on Centres of movement. Tracks & Headquarters. Cooperation of all guns on S.O.S. lines with Artillery Counter Preparation. 8500 rounds fired.	1/2/1
	26.2.18		Harassing fire throughout the night - annual all Guns fired in cooperation with Artillery Counter Preparation on S.O.S. lines 31750 rounds fired.	4/4